ARCHABET

ARCHABET
An Architectural Alphabet

Photographs by Balthazar Korab

National Trust for Historic Preservation

THE PRESERVATION PRESS

FOREWORD

Like fine paintings and old friends, the best buildings are those that continually divulge surprises. Architectural surprises may be built in by the architect or builder, but at least half of the responsibility for finding pleasurable details in buildings rests firmly with us, the viewers and users. It is up to us to look for the delights that architecture offers beyond its larger role as shelter for our activities. And there are many ways of looking at architecture — through styles and materials, through form and function, through architects and history. One way to seek out the pleasures of buildings is to make a game of it. Here we have found an alphabet in architecture, seen through the eyes of an artist. This is only one way to view architecture, and only one of many alphabets that can be found hidden among the buildings that surround us, but it proves how rich even the simplest-seeming structures can be. To see architecture is to appreciate it, and to appreciate it is to want to save and savor those specimens that continue to give delight.

DIANE MADDEX

P R E F A C E

Under huge chestnut trees, in a formidable brick
school, I learned my ABCs from a teacher who
carved letters on the blackboard with squeaky chalk. Long
on the road since then, I have met other symbols from
other worlds: elegant white characters on a 15-story
red scroll on my Shanghai hotel, tiny wedge-shaped
Sumerian cuneiforms, arabesques caked with whitewash
on mosques in Yemen — all with messages, but not for me.
S.P.Q.R. inscribed in the streets of Rome, illuminated
medieval manuscripts, Rimbaud's colored poetry — these
still hold the most magic for me and are the alphabets of
my world. When converted to musical notation, letters
are charged with even richer emotional content. Indeed,
the basic purpose of the letter is to convert sound,
whether speech or music, into a visible mark. Letters have
been the link between two main motifs of the human
experience, reason and emotions. Thus, let our letters here
be the link between us and music of another kind:
the frozen music, architecture.

BALTHAZAR KORAB

What is architecture anyway? Is it the vast collection of the various buildings which have been built to please the varying tastes of the various lords of mankind? I think not. No, I know that architecture is life, or at least it is life itself taking form and therefore it is the truest record of life as it was lived in the world yesterday, as it is lived today or ever will be lived. So architecture I know to be a Great Spirit. It can never be something which consists of the buildings which have been built by man on earth. . . . Architecture is that great living creative spirit which from generation to generation, from age to age, proceeds, persists, creates, according to the nature of man, and his circumstances as they change. That is really architecture.

FRANK LLOYD WRIGHT

A

Learning to look is a pleasure;
the buildings will embrace your eyes.

JUDITH LYNCH WALDHORN

B

Architecture begins where engineering ends.

WALTER GROPIUS

C

It is not enough to *see* architecture;
you must experience it.

STEEN EILER RASMUSSEN

D

The art of building, or architecture,
is the beginning of all the arts that lie
outside the person.

Havelock Ellis

E

Architecture, simply and
immediately perceived, is a combination,
revealed through light and shade,
of spaces, of masses, and of lines.

GEOFFREY SCOTT

F

Architecture can reach out beyond
the period of its birth, beyond the social
class that called it into being,
beyond the style to which it belongs.

SIGFRIED GIEDION

G

All styles are good except the boring kind.

VOLTAIRE

H

Well-building hath three conditions:
Commodity, Firmness, and Delight.

<small>Sir Henry Wotton</small>

I

Ornament if organic was never
on the thing but *of* it. . . .

FRANK LLOYD WRIGHT

J

God is in the detail.

Ludwig Mies van der Rohe

K

Form ever follows function.

Louis Henri Sullivan

L

All architecture is shelter;
all great architecture is the design
of space that contains, cuddles, exalts,
or stimulates the persons in that space.

PHILIP JOHNSON

M

Consider . . . the momentous event
in architecture when the wall parted
and the column became.

LOUIS I. KAHN

N

We shape our buildings,
and afterwards our buildings shape us.

WINSTON S. CHURCHILL

Form is not the aim of our work,
but only the result. Form, by itself,
does not exist.

LUDWIG MIES VAN DER ROHE

P

When we build, let us think
that we build for ever.

John Ruskin

Less is more.

Ludwig Mies van der Rohe

R

I like complexity and contradiction
in architecture. . . . I am for messy vitality
over obvious unity. . . . I am for richness
of meaning rather than clarity of
meaning; for the implicit function
as well as the explicit function.

ROBERT VENTURI

S

I call architecture frozen music.

JOHANN WOLFGANG VON GOETHE

T

Architecture is the masterly,
correct and magnificent play of volumes
brought together in light.

LE CORBUSIER

U

Architecture, like music, must be a part
of the composer, but it must also transcend
him to give something to music
or architecture itself. Mozart is not only
Mozart, but music.

Louis I. Kahn

V

We may live without her [architecture], and worship without her, but we cannot remember without her.

John Ruskin

W

One of modern architecture's greatest
failings has been its lack of interest
in the relationship of the building
to the sky. One doubts that a poem was
ever written to a flat-roofed building
silhouetted against the setting sun.

PAUL RUDOLPH

X

Architecture occurs when a building
and a person like each other.

WILLIAM WAYNE CAUDILL,
WILLIAM MERRIWEATHER PENA
and PAUL KENNON

Architecture, unlike other arts,
is not an escape from, but an acceptance of,
the human condition, including its many
frailties as well as the technical advances
of its scientists and engineers.

Pietro Belluschi

Z

Let us, while waiting for new monuments, preserve the ancient monuments.

VICTOR HUGO

ARCHABET

A Gothic Revival house,
Romeo, Mich.

B Sherman Minton Bridge over
the Ohio River between Louisville,
Ky., and New Albany, Ind.

C Interior of the cupola
at Longwood, Natchez, Miss.

D Good Luck gas station,
Dallas, Tex.

E Split rail fence
at Meffords Fort, Washington, Ky.

F Sawn-wood porch,
Monroe, Mich.

G Honolulu House,
Marshall, Mich.

H Donald Boudeman House,
Kalamazoo, Mich.

I Silos on a farm,
Monroe, Mich.

J Huntington House,
Howell, Mich.

K Abandoned gravel pit,
Oxford, Mich.

L Mitchell-Ogé House,
San Antonio, Tex.

M Rotunda of the Minnesota
State Capitol, St. Paul, Minn.

N Half-timbered house,
Old Salem, N.C.

O Gate near the Mississippi
River in Louisiana

P Lamp post at the Kingswood
School, Bloomfield Hills, Mich.

Q Windmill near a farmhouse,
Fenton, Mich.

R Sawyer House,
Monroe, Mich.

S Balcony grillwork
in the Vieux Carre,
New Orleans, La.

T Entrance portico
of the Cranbrook Art Academy,
Bloomfield Hills, Mich.

U Porch of the Tampa
Bay Hotel, Tampa, Fla.

V Old brick paving,
Savannah, Ga.

W Chapel of the Air
Force Academy,
Colorado Springs, Colo.

X Door of a house,
Monroe, Mich.

Y Gothic Revival house,
Washington, Ky.

Z Cast-iron stairway
in the City Hall,
Bay City, Mich.

QUOTATION SOURCES

Opening   "What Is Architecture." In *An Organic Architecture*, by Frank Lloyd Wright. 1939. 3rd ed. Cambridge: MIT Press, 1970.

A   *A Gift to the Street*, by Carol Olwell and Judith Lynch Waldhorn. 1976. Reprint. New York: St. Martin's Press, 1983.

B   Speech by Walter Gropius, Harvard Department of Architecture, 1938. See *Architects on Architecture: New Directions in America*, by Paul Heyer. 1966. Rev. ed. New York: Walker, 1978.

C   *Experiencing Architecture*, by Steen Eiler Rasmussen. Cambridge: MIT Press, 1959.

D   *The Dance of Life*, by Havelock Ellis. 1923. Reprint. Westport, Conn.: Greenwood Press, 1973.

E   *The Architecture of Humanism: A Study in the History of Taste*, by Geoffrey Scott. 1914, 1924. Reprint. New York: W. W. Norton, 1974.

F   *Space, Time and Architecture: The Growth of a New Tradition*, by Sigfried Giedion. Cambridge, Mass.: Harvard University Press, 1941.

G   "L'Enfant Prodigue," by Voltaire. 1736. In *Le Theatre de Voltaire*, edited by Theodore Besterman. Oxford: Voltaire Foundation, 1967.

H   After Vitruvius, *The Ten Books on Architecture*, Book 1, chapter iii. *The Elements of Architecture*, by Sir Henry Wotton. 1624. Reprint. Norwood, N.J.: Walter J. Johnson, 1970.

I   *A Testament*, by Frank Lloyd Wright. New York: Horizon Press, 1957.

J   Personal motto of Ludwig Mies van der Rohe. See "Mies van der Rohe," by Ludwig Glaeser. In *Macmillan Encyclopedia of Architects*, vol. 3, edited by Adolf K. Placzek. New York: Free Press, Macmillan, 1982.

K   "The Tall Office Building Artistically Considered," by Louis Henri Sullivan. *Lippincott's Magazine*, March 1896.

L   "What Makes Me Tick," speech by Philip Johnson, Columbia University, 1975. In *Philip Johnson: Writings*. New York: Oxford University Press, 1979.

M   *Between Silence and Light: Spirit in the Architecture of Louis I. Kahn,* by John Lobell. Boulder, Colo.: Shambhala Publications, 1979.

N   Speech by Winston S. Churchill, October 28, 1943. See *Winston S. Churchill: His Complete Speeches, 1897–1963,* edited by Robert Rhodes James. New York: Chelsea House, 1974.

O   Ludwig Mies van der Rohe, 1923. See *Mies van der Rohe,* by Werner Blaser. 1947. Rev. ed. New York: Praeger Publishers, 1978.

P   *The Seven Lamps of Architecture,* by John Ruskin. 1849. Reprint. New York: Farrar, Straus and Giroux, 1961.

Q   Personal motto of Ludwig Mies van der Rohe. See *Mies van der Rohe,* by Philip Johnson. 1947. New York: Museum of Modern Art, 1978.

R   *Complexity and Contradiction in Architecture,* by Robert Venturi. New York: Museum of Modern Art, 1966.

S   Letter from Goethe to Eckermann, February 4, 1829.

T   *Vers une Architecture,* by Le Corbusier. 1922. Paris: Arthaud, 1977.

U   *Between Silence and Light: Spirit in the Architecture of Louis I. Kahn,* by John Lobell. Boulder, Colo.: Shambhala Publications, 1979.

V   *The Seven Lamps of Architecture,* by John Ruskin. 1849. Reprint. New York: Farrar, Straus and Giroux, 1961.

W   "Paul Rudolph." In *Architects on Architecture: New Directions in America,* by Paul Heyer. 1966. Rev. ed. New York: Walker, 1978.

X   *Architecture and You: How to Experience and Enjoy Buildings,* by William Wayne Caudill, William Merriweather Pena and Paul Kennon. New York: Whitney Library of Design, 1978.

Y   "Pietro Belluschi." In *Architects on Architecture: New Directions in America,* by Paul Heyer. 1966. Rev. ed. New York: Walker, 1978.

Z   Victor Hugo, 1832.

The Preservation Press
National Trust for Historic Preservation
1785 Massachusetts Avenue, N.W.
Washington, D.C. 20036

The National Trust for Historic Preservation in the United States is the only private, nonprofit national organization chartered by Congress to encourage public participation in the preservation of sites, buildings and objects significant in American history and culture. Support is provided by membership dues, endowment funds, contributions and grants from federal agencies, including the U.S. Department of the Interior, under provisions of the National Historic Preservation Act of 1966. For information about membership and a complete list of other Preservation Press books, write to the National Trust at the above address.

ARCHABET was developed and edited by Diane Maddex, editor, Preservation Press books. Gretchen Smith, associate editor, and Helen Cook, administrative assistant, assisted with the production.

The book was designed by Marc Alain Meadows and Robert Wiser, Meadows & Wiser, Washington, D.C.

Type for the titles was composed in phototypositor Centaur by Phil's Photo, Inc., Washington, D.C., and for the text in Alphatype Centaurus by Harlowe Typography, Cottage City, Md. These typefaces were derived from a font designed by Bruce Rogers in 1915 for the Montague Press. The book was printed on 100-pound Mohawk Superfine by Wolk Press, Woodlawn, Md., and bound by Bookcrafters, Columbia, Md.

Printed in the United States of America

88 87 86 85   4 3 2 1

Library of Congress Cataloging in Publication Data

Korab, Balthazar.
    Archabet: an architectural alphabet.

    1. Buildings—United States—Pictorial
works.   2. Photography, Architectural.   I. Title.
NA705.K615 1985   779'.4'0924   84-26335
ISBN 0-89133-117-4

Twas the Night Before Christmas

Clement C. Moore

illustrated by Elena Almazova & Vitaly Shvarov

Grafton and Scratch
PUBLISHERS

'Twas the night before Christmas,
when all through the house,
not a creature was stirring,
not even a mouse.

The stockings were hung
by the chimney with care,
in hopes that St. Nicholas
soon would be there.

The children were nestled
all snug in their beds,
while visions of sugar plums
danced in their heads.

And Mama in her kerchief,
and I in my cap,
had just settled down
for a long winter's nap.
When out on the lawn
there arose such a clatter,
I sprang from the bed
to see what was the matter.

Away to the window I flew like a flash,
tore open the shutters and threw up the sash.

The moon on the crest of the new-fallen snow,
gave the lustre of midday to objects below.
When, what to my wondering eyes should appear,
but a miniature sleigh, and eight tiny reindeer.

With a little old driver, so lively and quick,
I knew in a moment it must be St. Nick.

More rapid than eagles his coursers they came,
and he whistled, and shouted, and called them by name.

"Now Dasher, now Dancer, now Prancer and Vixen!
On Comet, on Cupid, on Donner and Blitzen!
To the top of the porch, to the top of the wall!
Now dash away, dash away, dash away all!"

As dry leaves that before the wild hurricane fly,
when they meet with an obstacle, mount to the sky,
so up to the house-top the coursers they flew,
with a sleigh full of toys and St. Nicholas too.

And then in a twinkling, I heard on the roof,
the prancing and pawing of each little hoof.
As I drew in my head, and was turning around,
down the chimney St. Nicholas came with a bound.

He was dressed all in fur, from his head to his foot,
and his clothes were all tarnished with ashes and soot.

A bundle of toys he had flung on his back,
and he looked like a peddler just opening his pack.

His eyes how they twinkled!
His dimples how merry!
His cheeks were like roses,
his nose like a cherry!
His droll little mouth
was drawn up like a bow,
and the beard of his chin
was as white as the snow.

He had a broad face and a little round belly,
that shook when he laughed, like a bowlful of jelly.

He was chubby and plump, a right jolly old elf
and I laughed when I saw him, in spite of myself.
A wink of his eye and a twist of his head,
soon gave me to know I had nothing to dread.

He spoke not a word, but went straight to his work,
and filled all the stockings, then turned with a jerk,

and laying his finger aside of his nose,
and giving a nod, up the chimney he rose.

He sprang to his sleigh, to his team gave a whistle,
and away they all flew like the down of a thistle.
But I heard him exclaim, as he drove out of sight,

"Happy Christmas to all, and to all a good night."

Published simultaneously in the USA and in Canada in 2012 by Grafton and Scratch Publishers AtlasBooks Distribution

Contact us by e-mail:

publisher@TwasTheNightBeforeChristmas.ca

Visit us:
www.TwasTheNightBeforeChristmas.ca
www.BooksThatFit.com
www.goodreads.com

Also available in e-book formats, including enhanced version with audio and interaction. A softcover edition is available for nonprofit agencies through the offices of the publisher.

Follow us **@twas4kids**

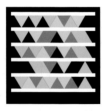 Find us
www.facebook.com/TwasTheNightBeforeChristmas

Printed in Canada on FSC ® certified paper made by New Page, Wisconsin, USA.

10 9 8 7 6 5 4 3 2 1

Book design by Elisa Gutiérrez

LIBRARY AND ARCHIVES CANADA CATALOGUING IN PUBLICATION

Moore, Clement Clarke, 1779-1863
    Twas the night before
Christmas / Clement C. Moore ; edited
by Santa Claus for the benefit of children of the 21st century.

Issued also in electronic format.
ISBN 978-0-9879023-0-6 (bound).--ISBN 978-0-9879023-1-3 (pbk.)

    I. Title.

PS2429.M5N5
2012   j811'.2   C2012-901278-5

LIBRARY AND ARCHIVES CANADA CATALOGUING IN PUBLICATION

Moore, Clement Clarke, 1779-1863
    Twas the night before
Christmas [electronic resource] / Clement
C. Moore ; edited by Santa Claus for the benefit of children of the 21st century.

Electronic monograph.
Issued also in print format.
ISBN 978-0-9879023-2-0 (ebook).--ISBN 978-0-9879023-3-7 (PDF)

    I. Title.

PS2429.M5N5
2012   j811'.2   C2012-901279-3

BREAKTHROUGH

ELECTRICITY

Tony Hooper

RSVP

**RAINTREE
STECK-VAUGHN**
P U B L I S H E R S
The Steck-Vaughn Company

Austin, Texas

Originated by Zoë Books Limited
Design: Pardoe Blacker
Cover Design: Scott Melcer
Picture Research: Sarah Staples
Illustrations: Arcana
Editors: Joe Degnan, Helene Resky
Consultant: Dr. Skipp Tullen
Electronic Production: Scott Melcer
Project Manager: Joyce Spicer

Library of Congress Cataloging-in-Publication Data

Hooper, Tony.
    Electricity / Tony Hooper.
        p.   cm. — (Breakthrough)
    Includes index.
    Summary: Surveys major breakthroughs in the science of electricity, from magnetism and electric motors to the electroscope and superconductivity.
    ISBN 0-8114-2334-4
    1. Electricity — Juvenile literature. 2. Electricity — History — Juvenile literature. [1. Electricity] I. Title. II. Series.
    QC527.2.H66   1994
    537—dc20   92-17023
                                                            CIP
                                                            AC

Printed and bound in the United States
1 2 3 4 5 6 7 8 9 0 VHP 99 98 97 96 95 94 93

Photograph acknowledgments
Cover photography clockwise from top right: Science Photo Library; ZEFA; Mary Evans Picture Library; Science Photo Library; © Joe Bator/The Stock Market.

The publishers wish to acknowledge, with thanks, the following photographic sources: 4 Ann Ronan; 5t Mary Evans Picture Library; 5b Trevor Hill; 6 Ann Ronan; 7t The Mansell Collection; 7b, 9t Ann Ronan; 9b, 10 Science Photo Library; 11 Ann Ronan; 12 Mary Evans Picture Library; 13 Ann Ronan; 16, 18 Mary Evans Picture Library; 19t, 19b Ann Ronan; 20, 21, 22, 23 The Mansell Collection; 24, 26 Ann Ronan; 27 The Mansell Collection; 28 Philip Sauvain; 29 The Mansell Collection; 30, 32, 33 Ann Ronan; 34 ZEFA Picture Library; 35 Mary Evans Picture Library; 37t GEC; 37b Science Photo Library; 38 NHPA; 40 UPI/Bettmann; 41t Texas Instruments; 41b, 42l, 42r Science Photo Library.

Contents

Early Ideas

In ancient Greece and Rome, groups of people liked to meet to discuss their views on different aspects of life. These philosophers believed that any question about the world, or the people and animals that lived in it, could be answered by reasoning alone. Since they relied on reasoning alone, they did not test their ideas to determine whether any were false. Many of the ideas, or **theories**, that they thought were true were later discovered to be quite wrong. However, for thousands of years many of their theories were accepted as the basis of science.

In the 16th century, lodestones were used as magnets and in compasses. Here, the suspended lodestone is attracting an iron lock and key. The other lodestones have been fitted or carved with pointers to show that they always line up in the same direction.

ATTRACTIVE STONES

One of the many mysteries that the philosophers studied was the curious power some stones had to draw toward themselves, or **attract**, the metal iron. These stones were first noticed over 3,000 years ago in Asia Minor (present-day Turkey). These minerals were called lodestones, and they were found near the town of Magnesia. This is why the mysterious power of attraction came to be called **magnetism**.

In 600 B.C. a Greek named Thales of Miletus referred to the ability of a **resin**, called amber, to attract light objects, such as lint or hair, when rubbed against cloth. He wondered what power made the amber act in this way.

Why lodestones attracted iron and why amber attracted lint puzzled philosophers for a long time. It took hundreds of years before anyone realized that the answers to these two questions had anything in common.

BREAKTHROUGH AND INSIGHT

Science often appears to progress in a series of sudden discoveries. These breakthroughs sometimes change people's way of thinking completely. However, breakthroughs are only possible when scientists carry out careful research and make logical deductions from their observations. This is true even when a chance observation leads to an idea, or **insight**, about nature.

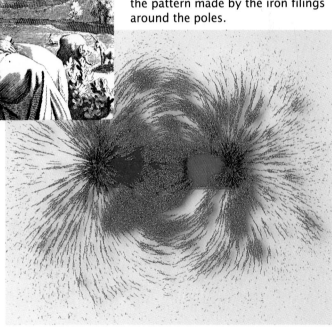

LUCRETIUS

Lucretius was a Roman philosopher who lived between 100 B.C. and 55 B.C. He belonged to a group of people who thought that all knowledge could be gained from the senses of sight, sound, smell, taste, and touch. He wrote a long poem *On the Nature of Things*. This work includes ideas about things being made of tiny particles, or **atoms**, the evolution of plants and animals, and the limitless extent of the universe. All of these ideas are recognizable today, but many of his other ideas have not stood the test of time. Lucretius based his ideas of magnetism on those of Empedocles, a philosopher who had lived about 300 years earlier. They both thought that magnetic stones sent out a stream of particles that entered tiny, invisible holes in iron. The particles drove out the air from these holes, and the iron was moved towards the **magnet** by the movement of the air, like a ship is blown by the wind.

Lucretius was also the first person to notice that iron filings fall into a regular pattern when they are close to a magnet, such as a lodestone.

The poles of this bar magnet are colored red and blue. You can see the pattern made by the iron filings around the poles.

ELECTRICITY

The study of electricity has provided many discoveries. One of these is that light and **radio waves** are just two versions of the same thing. Another is the discovery of the atomic structure of matter. These two discoveries have enabled us to make the **electronic** microchip, which has had an enormous influence and application in many different aspects of science and technology, including the widespread use of powerful computers at work and at home.

These discoveries have also given us the tools needed to increase our understanding of how the universe works. Scientists can look at individual atoms using an **electron** microscope, and astronomers use radio telescopes to study planets and distant stars in more detail than ever before.

Fossil fuels are increasingly becoming more scarce and more precious. Eventually nuclear **fusion** may provide electrical power for the future.

From Religion to Science

During the Middle Ages, the Christian religion gradually became very powerful in Europe. The leaders of the Christian church had decided which ideas and beliefs people were allowed to have. The leaders would not allow anyone to talk about ideas that were different from those taught by the church. The church taught that God created everything in seven days and that He was directly responsible for everything that happened. This conflicted with the theories of the philosophers of earlier times. However, if anyone questioned the teachings of the church, they could be tortured or killed.

This picture shows the famous 18th-century French chemist, Lavoisier, doing experiments that led to the discovery of the gas oxygen. He was an organized experimenter who built on the work of the first scientific experimenters of the 16th and 17th centuries.

SEEKING KNOWLEDGE

During the 1400s, the control of the church began to weaken. People become much more interested in learning, and many universities and new schools were set up. This period saw the first stirrings of what we now call science, but scientific thought still reflected the ideas of the ancient Greeks. These ideas were widely accepted until well into the 1500s. From 1500 to 1700, people began to challenge these ideas and to carry out tests, or **experiments**, to find out if their ideas were right or wrong.

Early Explanations of Magnetism

The first great thinkers were so puzzled by magnets that they could think of few natural explanations for them. Not much progress was made in understanding magnetism until the Middle Ages. A Roman named Pliny suggested that magnets had a soul and "attracted" iron just as we are attracted to those we like and love. Philosophers in the Middle Ages still clung to the idea of a soul, to a kind of "animal magnetism." They largely ignored the theories suggested by Lucretius, and magnets were widely thought to be magical and to be able to heal.

This early magnetic dip circle was used to measure angles of inclination all over the world.

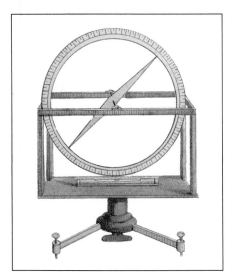

The behavior of magnets

Like poles repel.

Opposite poles attract.

PEREGRINUS'S EXPERIMENTS

In his experiments Peregrinus used magnetic needles. He saw that a floating magnetic needle always pointed in a north and south direction, toward the north and south **poles** of the Earth, so each end of the magnet became known as a pole. Peregrinus also found that when a second floating magnet was brought close to the first magnet, the **opposite poles** were attracted toward each other, and the **like poles** were pushed away, or repelled. In his next experiment, Peregrinus moved a magnetic needle over the surface of a ball-shaped magnet and noticed that the needle was most strongly attracted near the magnet's poles.

Finally, he broke a magnet in half and found each half acted as a complete magnet. He now had four poles instead of two! Due to this early work, Peregrinus has been called the "Father of Magnetism." Unfortunately, at that time, no one took any notice of his ideas.

Using Magnets

During the 1400s and 1500s, people began to take a wider interest in natural phenomenon. Several discoveries were made in the field of magnetism by sailors using magnetic compasses.

The sailors found that their needle magnets did not point exactly to true north but to a point nearby, **magnetic north**. The angle between true north and magnetic north is called the angle of declination. This angle varies from place to place on the surface of the Earth. In addition, it changes very slowly over time.

Sailors also noticed that, as they sailed around the world, the vertical angle (with respect to the horizon) made by their magnets changed. This variation is known as inclination. Christopher Columbus noticed this effect while he was making his first voyage to the Americas in 1492. This knowledge was largely ignored until 1581 when Robert Norman, an English navigator, made measurements of declination and inclination from many places in the world.

hanging bar magnet

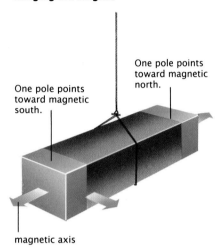

One pole points toward magnetic north.

One pole points toward magnetic south.

magnetic axis

The magnet will always line up in the same direction.

The Earth's magnetism

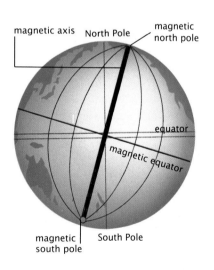

magnetic axis North Pole magnetic north pole

equator

magnetic equator

magnetic south pole South Pole

The magnetic north and south poles are not in the same place as the geographic North and South Poles. Also, the magnetic poles move over the centuries.

Measuring inclination

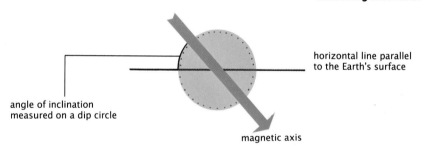

horizontal line parallel to the Earth's surface

angle of inclination measured on a dip circle

magnetic axis

Old wives' tales

Many people still believed that magnetism was like an emotion and that magnets had souls. They thought that magnets could grow old, like us, and as the magnets aged, their attraction to iron grew less. It was also thought that magnetic needles turned instinctively, like a wolf returning to its den.

An Italian, Giambattista della Porta, found that magnets do not get heavier after they have been left in iron filings. From this result he came to the conclusion that the magnet's "soul" did not eat iron! Della Porta also had a theory about amber. He thought that the amber's attraction for lint was due to an unseen, fatty substance that came out of amber when it was rubbed. Light, dry bits of lint would then stick to this fatty substance.

This later electroscope was built by Volta. The top plate has a handle. After the top plate had been charged with electricity by rubbing, it was moved close to the other plate. The thin pieces of metal foil in the center of the glass bulb moved further apart as the plates got closer. (See more details on page 12.)

NEW CONCEPTS

William Gilbert continued Petrus Peregrinus's work with spherical magnets. Gilbert proposed that a round magnet would act just like a miniature version of the Earth with **rays of magnetic force** spreading out from the magnet. Gilbert then studied these rays by looking at the way an iron needle behaved when it was moved around his magnetic model of the Earth. He found that the strength of magnetic attraction fell as the needle moved farther away, but it never reduced to zero. Gilbert formed the concepts of a real, or physical, force and that there was an area of magnetic force, or **magnetic field**, around each magnet. Inclination is the angle of the Earth's magnetic field with respect to the surface at a given location.

WILLIAM GILBERT

The first person to make a real distinction between electrical attraction and magnetism was William Gilbert, who was physician to Queen Elizabeth I of England. The study of electricity can be said to have started as a separate science with the publication of Gilbert's book *De Magnete* in 1600.

Gilbert was aware of Petrus Peregrinus's work and found that amber was not the only substance that could be made to attract objects after being rubbed. Gilbert wrongly imagined that when you rubbed amber, it breathed out something that attracted objects by a sort of sucking action. Gilbert called this attraction *electricity* after the Greek word for amber, *elektron*. Gilbert also developed a device he called an **electroscope**, which was the first instrument built to investigate electricity. Using the electroscope, Gilbert found that when a piece of rubbed amber was brought near to a light, wooden pointer resting on a **pivot**, the pointer revolved.

Magnetic field lines

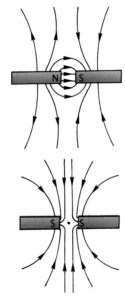

Magnetic field lines form when opposite and like poles are put together.

A neutral point, or point of zero magnetism, occurs where two or more magnetic fields have an equal but opposing effect.

weak magnetic field

strong magnetic field (Arrows show lines of magnetic force.)

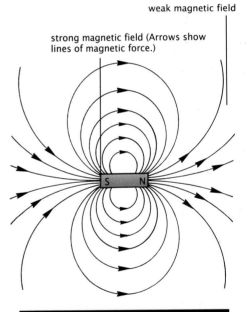

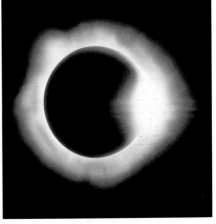

The corona of the sun can be seen from the Earth during a total eclipse. The gas particles stream out along magnetic lines of force to make the "solar wind."

Magnetism and Electricity

William Gilbert and other early students of electricity did much to advance the way people thought about electricity, but they made no measurements or did any experiments to back up their theories. They still held on to the belief that the magnetic forces were caused by an animallike attraction.

RENÉ DESCARTES

René Descartes was a French philosopher who was born in 1596, a few years before William Gilbert's death. He admired much of Gilbert's work. However, Descartes believed that the attractions had a mechanical explanation and had nothing to do with souls or animal attraction. Descartes was the first to make a drawing of the lines of magnetic force and explain the variation in magnetic declination by deciding, wrongly, that it was due to the mining of lodestone, which changed the distribution of the magnetic material.

ROBERT BOYLE

Around 1660, Robert Boyle, a British philosopher and chemist, made an important contribution to knowledge about electricity and magnetism when he showed that magnetic attraction did not depend on air to transmit its effects. He did this by putting a pivoting magnetic needle in a glass bottle that he then joined to a **vacuum pump** so that he could take the air out of the bottle.

Boyle then used a magnet outside the bottle to show that the needle moved in exactly the same way as it did when the bottle was full of air. He also showed that, when two objects are rubbed together, they have an electrical attraction for each other. This is called **static electricity**.

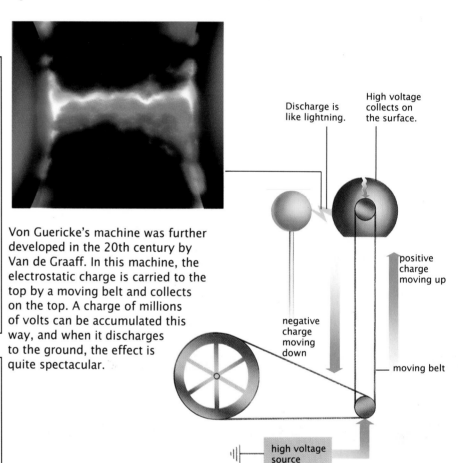

Von Guericke's machine was further developed in the 20th century by Van de Graaff. In this machine, the electrostatic charge is carried to the top by a moving belt and collects on the top. A charge of millions of volts can be accumulated this way, and when it discharges to the ground, the effect is quite spectacular.

Discharge is like lightning.

High voltage collects on the surface.

positive charge moving up

negative charge moving down

moving belt

high voltage source

THE FIRST ELECTRICAL MACHINE

The first real experimenter in electricity was a German named Otto von Guericke. He invented the first electrical machine during the mid-1600s. This was made from a sulfur sphere that could be turned by hand and rubbed to make sparks. Von Guericke was an excellent experimenter and made many demonstrations of electrical attraction and **repulsion** on the electrification of a cotton thread along with many other effects.

At the end of the 1600s some work was done by the Dutch astronomer and physicist, Christiaan Huygens. He made clear distinctions between the forces of magnetism, electricity, and **gravity**, the force that attracts masses to each other.

Discoveries in Electricity in the 1700s

Unfortunately, Otto von Guericke's work was largely ignored, and the next important breakthrough was not to come until 1729 when the British physicist Stephen Gray discovered something by accident. Gray was experimenting with a glass tube that had been electrified by rubbing. The electrified tube had a cork in it. Gray already knew that the glass tube would attract a feather, but he was amazed to find that the cork also attracted the feather.

After this discovery, Gray, with the help of his friend Granvil Wheeler, did more experiments. When they fixed different threads (like silk) to the cork, they found that the attracting effect passed along, or was **conducted**, right to the end of the threads. However, the maximum distance of the conduction depended on the type of thread. Gray was eventually able to demonstrate that this attraction was still working at the end of a piece of wet thread that was 951 feet (290 m) long!

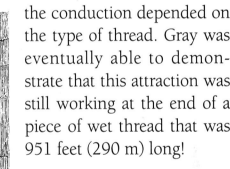

The artist has shown early experiments in which Stephen Gray passed electricity from a glass tube static electricity machine down 145 feet (45 meters) of a piece of thread. The static electricity was made by rubbing the cloth (in Gray's right hand) against the glass tube.

ELECTRICAL INDUCTION

Stephen Gray also carried out some experiments with a piece of lead that he hung from the ceiling. He discovered that when he moved an electrified glass tube close to (but not touching) the lead, the lead could attract tiny pieces of metal. The electrical effect had been transferred, or **induced**, into the lead without any physical contact. Gray was also the first to suggest that there was something in common between electrical sparks and lightning, although Benjamin Franklin is credited with this finding.

Allowing Electricity to Pass

Stephen Gray's work was extended in France by the chemist Charles Du Fay. The two men wrote regularly to each other and exchanged many ideas. In 1733, the results of Du Fay's experiments were published. He showed that some materials could *not* become electrified just by rubbing them.

Du Fay then demonstrated that some of these materials, such as metals, could have electricity transferred to them by induction provided the materials rested on or were surrounded by another material that *did not* become electrified, such as glass or sealing wax. These materials were known as **insulators**. Du Fay had discovered that some materials, **conductors**, were better at allowing the electrical effect to be transmitted than other materials (nonconductors, or insulators).

Charles Du Fay made many experiments with his electroscope, which he had previously **charged**. He noticed that, while some of the electrified substances, like glass and rock crystal, repelled the charged gold leaf, others, like amber, resin, and sealing wax, attracted the gold leaf.

A gold leaf electroscope

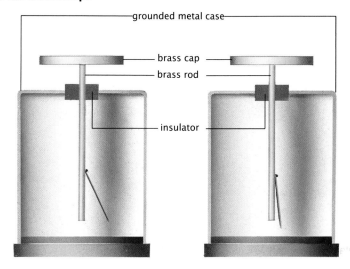

grounded metal case

brass cap

brass rod

insulator

piece of gold leaf repelled by rod when electricity is present

piece of gold leaf lying next to rod when electricity is not present

TWO TYPES OF ELECTRICITY?

Du Fay had originally expected that all the materials would behave like glass and repel the gold leaf. He decided that there must be two types of electricity. Although Du Fay did not fully understand, he was able to show that either type of electricity could pass by induction to insulated conducting objects.

Early Electrical Experiments

The only way the early scientists could produce electricity was by rubbing, or causing **friction**, on materials such as glass or resin rods. Otto von Guericke's experiments were rediscovered, and his electrical machine was introduced and improved. Most versions had a rotating glass tube or ball. The operator electrified the glass by holding his hand against the turning glass. Later versions used a leather strap to rub the glass, and the electricity was "collected" by a woven metal braid that "brushed" against the glass. By the mid-1700s, public demonstrations of machines making spectacular and noisy electrical sparks were very popular.

STORING ELECTRICITY

People had noticed that electricity gradually leaked away from an electrified body. In 1745, Ewald von Kleist, who was dean of the Cathedral of Kamin in Pomerania, wondered if this leakage was similar to water **evaporating** and whether it could be lessened if the electricity was stored in water in a glass bottle. He reasoned that as water cannot evaporate from a corked bottle, so electricity would not evaporate either.

Von Kleist filled a bottle with water and stuck a nail through the cork. Then, holding the bottle, he put the nail to the collector of his electrical machine. Later, he touched the nail to a grounded object and saw a strong spark! He also used his hand as the non-insulated body and felt a painful shock!

THE LEYDEN JAR

Ewald Von Kleist's experiment was repeated in the Netherlands by Pieter van Musschenbroek in 1746. Van Musschenbroek was a professor at Leyden University who immediately realized that Von Kleist had found a way of storing electricity. Within the year, electrical experimenters all over the world were using the Leyden jar and trying to understand how it worked.

Van Musschenbroek is shown here charging a glass jar holding water with electricity. The electrical machine is turned by a pulley system, and the electricity is made by rubbing the rotating sphere. Electricity is picked up by a chain touching the sphere and conducted to the jar by the iron bar hanging from insulating ropes.

The Electrical Circuit

In the mid-1700s, British physicist Sir William Watson noticed one other important point about the behavior of electricity. He performed some experiments with his electrical machine and two lines of people holding hands. They all stood on a waxed floor that insulated them from the ground. The person at the head of the first chain of people held the collector of an electrical machine. The person at the head of the second chain held on to a metal gun barrel.

Making a circuit

electrical machine

waxed floor acting as insulator

metal gun barrel

The circuit was completed when the people at the ends of the two lines joined hands because the metal gun barrel was touching the ground as was the other end of the electrical machine.

A SHOCKING EXPERIENCE

When the two people at the ends of the chains held hands, all the people in both chains felt an electric shock. Watson repeated his experiment and showed that people, although still holding hands, did not feel the shock unless they were in a **circuit**, or made a complete link between the source of the electricity and the metal.

Watson and his contemporaries had discovered many basic facts about the behavior of electricity. However, all these ideas and theories were so complicated and confusing that no one could develop a convincing and clear explanation for how electricity worked.

Benjamin Franklin

In the 1750s, Benjamin Franklin performed a series of experiments that advanced our knowledge about electricity. He was the first to understand that electricity was not actually made by friction but was pulled out, or **extracted**, as though it was already present in the rotating glass of the electrical machine.

To explain Charles Du Fay's "two types of electricity," Franklin used the terms **positive** and **negative** electricity, and showed that this meant that a body could have more electricity (or be electrified plus or positive) than another body (which would be electrified minus or negative). It was Franklin who first used the terms *charge* and *field*.

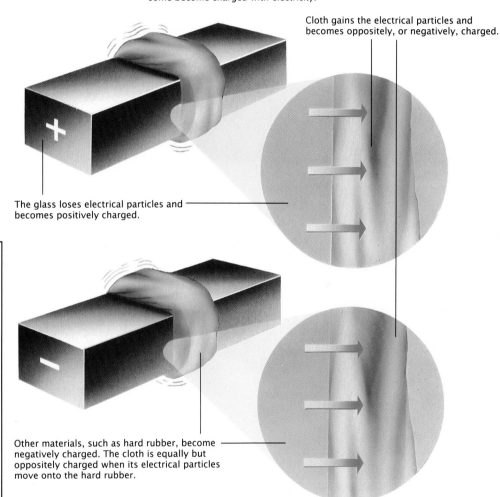

Static electricity When two materials are rubbed together, some become charged with electricity.

Cloth gains the electrical particles and becomes oppositely, or negatively, charged.

The glass loses electrical particles and becomes positively charged.

Other materials, such as hard rubber, become negatively charged. The cloth is equally but oppositely charged when its electrical particles move onto the hard rubber.

LIGHTNING IS ELECTRICITY

Benjamin Franklin, the well-known diplomat, played an important role in establishing the United States of America in the 1770s. He was an author and had a great interest in science, especially electricity. He invented many scientific terms still in use today. He also formed a solid foundation of ideas for other scientists.

In May 1752, during a thunderstorm, Franklin carried out a dangerous experiment when he flew a kite. He held the kite string, a short length of silk ribbon, in his hand, while the other end of the ribbon was tied to a key. When the kite string became wet, Franklin could draw sparks from the key to his free hand. This proved that lightning and electricity are related. Franklin could have been killed by the lightning! He went on to invent the lightning rod, which is a grounded metal rod fixed to the outside of buildings to carry the charge safely to earth.

SQUEEZING THE SPONGE

Franklin came to believe that his experiments showed that electricity existed in ordinary matter like water in a sponge. When you "squeezed" the "sponge" (for example, by rubbing the rotating glass ball of an electrical machine), the electricity came out. Franklin believed that electrical matter was different from ordinary matter. He thought that the tiny particles of electricity repelled each other, while the particles of ordinary matter attracted each other.

Early Electrical Measurements

Henry Cavendish, a British physicist, took Benjamin Franklin's work one step farther. Cavendish showed that when two objects were joined by a metal conducting wire and electrified, the distribution charge on each object depended on its shape and size even though they were electrified to the same degree. For example, on a metal object shaped like an egg, Cavendish found the highest concentration of charge on the pointed end. An object's electrical **potential** is related to the amount of electrical charge on it. We call the potential difference between two charged objects the **voltage**.

Henry Cavendish, the physicist who discovered electrical potential, was also a chemist. He discovered that water is a compound of hydrogen and oxygen.

Potential
The unit of potential difference is the volt.

Positive charge tends to move toward lower potential (B).

The position of A in an electric field gives it a higher potential than B.

There is a potential difference between points A and B.

Negative charge tends to move toward higher potential (A).

THE CAPACITOR

Cavendish also made some interesting discoveries when working with a device known as a capacitor, which is used for storing an electric charge. Capacitors are made from two plates of a metal, like tin. The plates are usually close to each other but separated by a thin layer of waxed paper or a similar insulating material. When the capacitor is electrified, it becomes charged with electricity. Cavendish discovered that the amount of electric charge the device could hold, or its capacitance, depended on the capacitance of the capacitor's plates and the type of insulating material separating the plates.

The capacitor

metal plates—The capacitance increased with their size.

Plate separator, or dielectric, made of insulating material. The kind of material used also affects the capacity.

electrical connections

The capacitance also grows larger as the gap between the plates gets smaller.

CHARLES COULOMB

Charles Coulomb was a French physicist who lived around the same time as Cavendish. Like him, Coulomb was a thorough experimenter. He trained as a mechanical engineer and only became interested in electricity in 1777, when he entered a public competition to make a better ship's compass.

SOME LAWS OF MAGNETISM

From the work that Charles Coulomb did, he concluded that the Earth has an even, or **uniform**, magnetic field. He also found that a magnet within that field will have a force acting on it that depends on the angle of the magnet with respect to the Earth's magnetic poles and the direction of the magnetic lines of force in the Earth's field. So, if the magnet could turn around its center, the magnetic lines of force would turn the magnet until it lined up with the Earth's field. Then the force on the magnet would fall to zero as the angle became zero.

VERY ACCURATE MEASUREMENTS

During the 1780s, Coulomb used an instrument known as the torsion balance that could measure tiny electrical forces. With this instrument, he made many important experiments in electrical repulsion and attraction. As a result, he was able to make accurate predictions and form general laws that others used to make further discoveries.

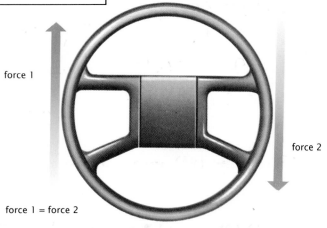

force 1

force 2

force 1 = force 2

The equal and opposite forces on a steering wheel cause it to turn.

Animal Electricity

In 1771, in Italy, an anatomist named Luigi Galvani made an exciting discovery. He was dissecting a dead frog in his laboratory when, by chance, one of his helpers touched a **nerve** in the frog's spine with a metal knife while the laboratory's version of von Guericke's electrical machine was operating. The leg twitched violently.

In 1780 Galvani carried out further experiments and found he was also able to make the legs move when he put a copper hook into the nerve and hung the hook from an iron rail. Galvani thought that the movement was caused by "animal electricity" that was stored in the frog, just as electricity was stored in a Leyden jar.

Volta's original pile had about 30 cells of copper and zinc separated by cardboard soaked in salt water. Later he used silver instead of copper and made cells in groups of 8. These could be connected together to make a battery as large as required.

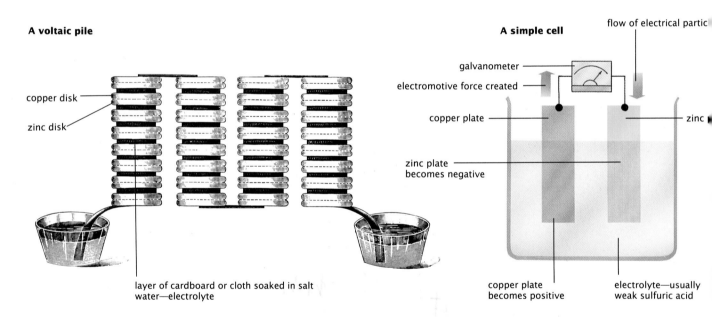

A voltaic pile

copper disk

zinc disk

layer of cardboard or cloth soaked in salt water—electrolyte

A simple cell

flow of electrical particles

galvanometer

electromotive force created

copper plate

zinc plate becomes negative

zinc

copper plate becomes positive

electrolyte—usually weak sulfuric acid

THE INVENTION OF THE BATTERY

Another Italian, Alessandro Volta, was a professor of physics at Pavia University at the same time that Galvani was a lecturer at Bologna University. Volta did not accept Galvani's idea of animal electricity. Volta thought that the movement was caused by a **reaction** between the two metals copper and iron.

Volta eventually put together a copper disk and a zinc disk separated by a cardboard disk soaked in salty water. This pair of disks with its separator is called a **cell**.

Volta built a pile of cells so that the copper and zinc disks were in contact. His original pile was made from 30 to 40 pairs of disks, always in the same order. This pile of cells produced, or **generated**, an electric

output. However, the electric output seemed to renew itself after each **discharge**.

Volta realized that this new form of electricity differed from the output of a Leyden jar because it was continuous. The Leyden jar output was always sudden and shocking! He took to calling the output of his pile a current of electricity, like the continuous flow of a river.

Splitting Up Water

The way the voltaic pile worked was not fully understood for a long time. In Italy, at the end of the 1700s, Giovanni Fabbroni had noticed that, when a plate of zinc and a plate of copper were immersed in water and connected by a conducting wire, the zinc plate became tarnished, or **oxidized**. He concluded that there must be something in common between this oxidization and the generation of electricity found in Volta's battery.

The next breakthrough was in Great Britain in 1800 when two chemists, Sir Anthony Carlisle and William Nicholson, were experimenting with the voltaic pile. They had connected wires to each end of the pile. The wires were put in water, and they saw that bubbles of gas appeared on the wires. They discovered that the bubbles were of different gases. Oxygen bubbles appeared at one wire while hydrogen appeared at the other. They decided that they had split water into its basic **elements**.

HUMPHRY DAVY

Another British chemist, Humphry Davy, expanded work on the voltaic pile still further. He refined Fabbroni's experiments and finally decided that the chemical changes seen in the oxidization of the zinc and in the release of hydrogen and oxygen were "somehow the cause of the electrical effect it produces." This effect is now known as the **electrolytic effect.** Davy's work was brought to the attention of the Royal Institution in London where, in 1801, at the age of 23, he was appointed professor of chemistry.

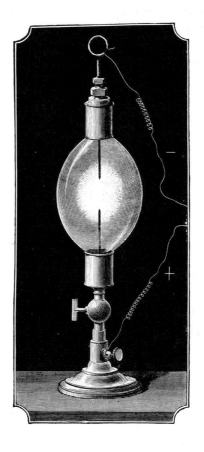

THE ELECTRIC ARC

Davy continued his investigation into Volta's battery and built a pile with 2,000 cells. Davy connected the battery to two pieces of charcoal, which is made of carbon. When the pieces were brought close to each other, the carbon caught fire. An extremely hot, bright flame shot from one end of the carbon to the other, making a glowing arc. This was the first demonstration of the **carbon arc** lamp that was to be widely used later for lights and for melting metals.

Davy enclosed his carbon rods in a glass globe and called it an electric egg. Because the carbon burned away very quickly, the gap between the two pieces of carbon had to be constantly adjusted. Later commercial versions of carbon arc lamps used graphite, a hard form of carbon, and motors to adjust the gap between the two pieces of carbon automatically.

The Magnetic Effects of Electricity

It has long been suspected that electrical and magnetic effects had something in common. However, it was not until 1819 that the Danish physicist, Hans Christian Ørsted, made a chance observation that gave scientists a clue to the relationship.

During a lecture to a small group of students, Ørsted closed, or completed, a battery circuit that allowed an electric current to pass through a wire. To his surprise, a nearby magnetic needle moved at the same time. Ørsted immediately realized that he had, at last, made a breakthrough in discovering the connection between electricity and magnetism. He set about doing a series of experiments to investigate the effect more thoroughly.

Ørsted is shown here, in this old engraving, demonstrating the deflection, or turning, of a magnetic needle when a current-carrying wire is moved close to it. The current is made by the simple battery in the glass jar on the right.

ELECTROMAGNETISM

Ørsted made a more powerful battery for his experiments. He was able to show that when the wire was above the needle and the current was switched on, the needle turned, or **deflected**, in one direction, and when the wire was under the needle, the needle deflected in the opposite direction. Ørsted concluded that these results could be explained if the force moving the magnetic needle was a magnetic force produced by the electricity in the wire. This magnetic effect reached into the surrounding space, or "field."

Ørsted's scientific experiments were published in Denmark on July 21, 1820. Many copies were sent to other leading scientists, such as Humphry Davy and his assistant, Michael Faraday.

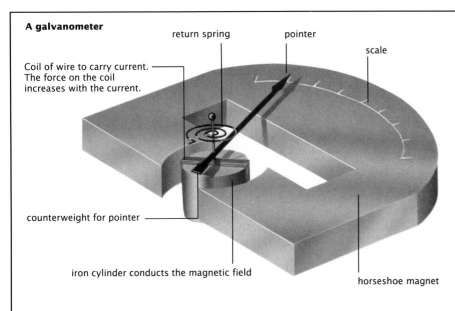

A galvanometer

return spring

pointer

scale

Coil of wire to carry current. The force on the coil increases with the current.

counterweight for pointer

iron cylinder conducts the magnetic field

horseshoe magnet

The current passing through the coil produces a turning force that is balanced by the forces produced by the magnet.

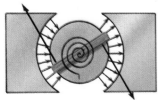

ANDRÉ AMPÈRE'S CONTRIBUTION

Ørsted's results caused a sensation and sparked off a wonderful period of discovery in electricity. Only one week after the news reached France, the physicist André Ampère showed that two **parallel** wires carrying electric currents would attract each other if the currents flowed in the same direction and repel each other when the currents flowed in different directions. In order to prove his **electrodynamic** law, Ampère invented an instrument that he called the galvanometer, after Luigi Galvani. His instrument had a simple conducting wire and a magnetic compass needle placed under the wire. The angle of deflection of the needle depended on the amount of current in the wire. The strength of the magnetic field produced by this current was measured in a unit later called an **ampere**, or **amp**.

The modern galvanometer measures current directly. The current passing through the coil makes the pointer deflect. The higher the current the more the pointer moves.

André-Marie Ampère

THE ELECTROMAGNET

In Germany, the physicist Johann Schweigger developed an improved version of the galvanometer in which he used a rectangular coil as a conductor to increase the movement of the needle. Schweigger used wire in his coil wrapped 100 times, which also multiplied the effect 100 times! This idea was taken further by William Sturgeon, a British physicist. He bent a soft iron bar into the form of a horseshoe. Then he insulated it from the electricity by covering it with a coat of varnish and wound a conducting wire around the horseshoe. When he passed an electric current through the wire, he was able to pick up an iron weight of 7.7 pounds (3.5 kg). This was the first **electromagnet**.

An electromagnet

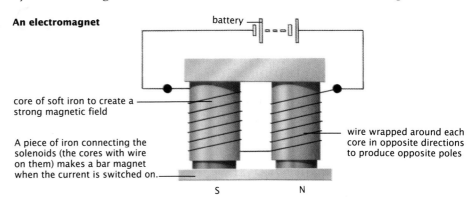

battery

core of soft iron to create a strong magnetic field

A piece of iron connecting the solenoids (the cores with wire on them) makes a bar magnet when the current is switched on.

wire wrapped around each core in opposite directions to produce opposite poles

S   N

Georg Ohm and Electric Currents

André Ampère had introduced the scientific world to the idea of electric current, and, in 1821, Humphry Davy had shown that the conducting ability of a wire depended on its thickness, or **cross section**. However, there was still no clear relation between the current and the potential difference, or voltage, of Volta's battery. This was because the batteries were too varied and primitive and could not supply a current that was steady enough to make accurate measurements possible.

In 1825, Georg Ohm, a German physicist, began his experiments to find the relationship between the current, voltage, and resistance of a circuit, using a voltaic pile. However, one year later he switched to using **thermoelectric junctions**, or couples. A thermocouple produces current that is dependent on the difference in temperature of the two junctions. So, if the temperature of one junction is known, the other temperature can be worked out by measuring the current in the circuit.

THE THERMOELECTRIC EFFECT

The thermoelectric effect (or Seebeck effect) was discovered in Germany in 1822 by Thomas Seebeck. Like Volta, Seebeck was experimenting with the effects created by joining together dissimilar metals, known as junctions, or couples.

Seebeck found that when he had two junctions connected together by a conductor, when each junction was kept at a different temperature, then a small electric current was generated. The amount of current depended on the difference in temperature between the two junctions. If the temperature difference was kept steady, then the current was steady, too. This was simple to do. One thermocouple was put into a container of ice, and the other thermocouple was put into a container of boiling water!

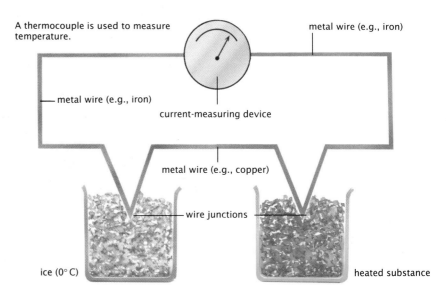

A thermocouple is used to measure temperature.

metal wire (e.g., iron)

metal wire (e.g., iron)

current-measuring device

metal wire (e.g., copper)

wire junctions

ice (0° C)

heated substance

MEASURING RESISTANCE

Ohm was able to measure the exact relationship between current, voltage, and resistance. Resistance is the tendency of a conductor to impede the flow of electricity. He showed that, in any particular circuit, the intensity of the electric current in the circuit was equal to the voltage divided by the total resistance. An **ohm** is the unit used as a measure of resistance.

The Genius of Faraday

In 1819, Michael Faraday became Humphry Davy's laboratory assistant at the Royal Institution in London. In 1804, at the age of 13, Faraday had been apprenticed as a bookbinder and soon became an avid reader of Davy's books and an amateur experimenter with electricity. He attended some of Davy's lectures and took notes, which he bound and presented to Davy. Davy was impressed by Faraday's grasp of his lectures and appointed him as his assistant.

Michael Faraday's work was wide-ranging and covered many scientific areas. Many practical electrical engineers seized on his ideas and then developed a whole range of products. Before his death in 1862, Faraday saw the introduction of commercial electric generators, alternators, motors, magnetos to produce an ignition spark in an engine, and carbon arc lighting (for the stage and for lighthouses), all of which had been made possible by his thoughts and experiments.

THE ELECTRIC MOTOR

In 1821, Michael Faraday repeated Hans Christian Ørsted's original experiment. Faraday concluded that the magnetic needle moved because its poles tended to travel around the wire carrying the current.

Within one week, he had completed a clever experiment to prove his theory. He had two bowls of the liquid metal mercury. In the center of one he placed an upright, or vertical, conductor touching the mercury and an upright magnet free to turn. In the center of the other bowl he placed a vertical magnet, and a free moving vertical conductor touched the mercury. The two vertical conductors were joined by a conductor. The magnets and the mercury were electrical conductors, too, so when a battery was attached to the magnets, the circuit was completed, and a current flowed. The floating magnet rotated around the fixed conductor, while the free conductor moved around the fixed magnet! The ability to use electricity and magnetism to cause rotation is the basis of electric motors. Faraday's discovery would change the world.

Faraday's Inventions

During the next ten years, although Michael Faraday was in regular contact with André Ampère, his main work was with his chemical experiments. However, Faraday thought that it was possible to produce electricity from magnetism and returned to experiments in electricity in 1831.

Over the course of five incredible months, from August to December, he discovered and invented the machines that enable us to generate **direct current (DC)**. He also invented the **alternator** to generate **alternating current (AC)**. This led him to invent the **transformer**, which enabled alternating currents to be produced with larger or smaller voltages. All commercial electricity generation today uses Faraday's discoveries.

THE COPPER PUZZLE

In 1824, François Arago, a French astronomer and physicist, found that the movement of a magnetic needle was quickly stopped, or damped, when it was suspended over a copper disk. This puzzled everybody because, although copper was a good conductor of electricity, it could not be permanently magnetized like iron. Also, when the copper disk was spun, it made the magnet move.

ELECTROMAGNETIC INDUCTION AND THE TRANSFORMER

Faraday thought that he had the answer to the copper puzzle and made an iron ring with two coils of insulated copper wire wound around the ring, opposite each other. He connected the ends of one coil together by a long piece of wire, which also passed over a magnetic needle 3 feet (1 m) away from the iron ring.

The second coil was connected to a battery by a switch, and when the switch was either opened (to break the circuit) or closed (to complete the circuit), the magnet moved! He also found that the movement was stronger if the second coil had more turns than the first coil. This was the first transformer and the first demonstration of how electrical induction works. The current was made to appear, or was induced, in the second circuit by the magnetic field produced by current in the first circuit.

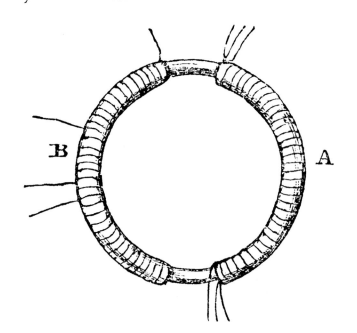

Faraday's first transformer was made from a 6-inch (15-cm) diameter iron ring wound with a number of insulated coils of wire that were joined together. When he connected a battery to one coil (B), he found that a current was formed in the other coils (A).

GENERATING ELECTRICITY

Faraday went on to experiment with a flattened wire coil. Part of the coil passed, as before, over a magnetic needle, but this time he moved the coil by hand between two opposite magnetic poles. Once again, the needle moved. Faraday had finally shown that electricity could be generated from magnetism.

A simple transformer

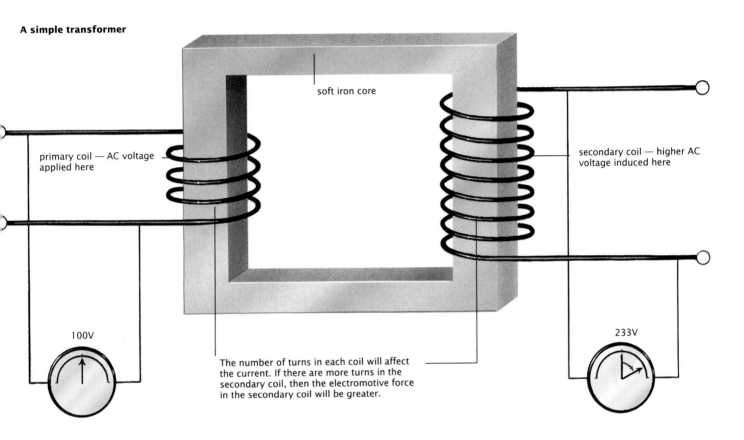

soft iron core

primary coil — AC voltage applied here

secondary coil — higher AC voltage induced here

The number of turns in each coil will affect the current. If there are more turns in the secondary coil, then the electromotive force in the secondary coil will be greater.

100V

233V

A modern transformer using alternating current and voltage. The ratio of the voltages at the input and output is proportional to the ratio of the number of turns in the primary and secondary coils. So if there are four turns on the primary and eight turns on the secondary, the secondary output voltage will be twice the primary input voltage.

CONTINUOUS CURRENT

Faraday continued his experiments but with a more powerful horseshoe magnet. He wanted to study Arago's results more closely and did an experiment in which a vertical copper disk was turned on a horizontal axle, between the poles of the horseshoe magnet. He placed sliding electrical **contacts** on the edge and the axle of the disk. While it turned, strong electric currents were generated in the copper disk. This was the first continuous current generator.

Faraday knew that all of these effects must be connected and that they obey some rule or law. He explained the effects by saying that induction depended on an **electromotive force**.

However, the results were not properly understood until 1832 when Joseph Henry finally discovered the effect called **self-induction**. This makes short-lived surges of current appear in a circuit when the current is either made or broken.

Faraday Looks at the Nature of Electricity

In 1832, Michael Faraday returned to his investigation of Alessandro Volta's battery. This time, Faraday was interested in the chemical changes that took place in the battery. He was convinced that each type of "Electricity, whatever may be its source, is identical in nature."

Faraday started by looking at what happened when an electric current passed through a liquid like salt water. Previous experimenters had shown that the water would be separated into its basic elements of hydrogen and oxygen. It was commonly supposed that this separation of salt water into hydrogen and oxygen only happened because the metal terminals of the battery, in contact with the salt water, attracted the elements. Faraday showed that this was wrong and that contact of the metal terminals with the salt water was not necessary.

Later experimenters found that, if they used a conducting liquid that had a metallic content, ions of the metal separated out of the liquid and covered, or plated, the **electrodes**. The electroplating process became very popular, and many cheap, ordinary metal objects (like knives, forks, and spoons) were plated with a thin layer of silver to make them look expensive.

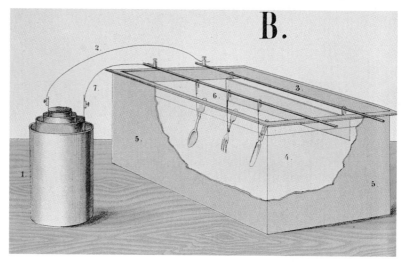

ELECTRICALLY CHARGED PARTICLES

Michael Faraday decided to ignore all previous ideas about why the water separated into its elements. To help him do this, he invented a new set of names for all the things he thought were involved. Faraday called the process **electrolysis** and invented the names **cathode**, to describe the terminal of a battery we mark with a minus sign, and **anode**, for the battery terminal marked with a plus sign. Faraday's experiments convinced him that, as a direct result of the current passing through it, the liquid separated into positively or negatively charged particles, which he called **ions**. The ions were then attracted to their oppositely charged battery terminal. So negative ions would be attracted to the anode, and positive ions would move toward the cathode. This was a revolutionary way of thinking, and it was vital to the development of our modern ideas about the nature of electricity and matter.

Later Ideas in Electricity

After 1840, electrical research concentrated on discovering a law of nature describing a force that could account for all of the electrical effects that had been discovered. Both Ampère's and Faraday's ideas were in the forefront of this effort, but their explanations, although useful, were divided and confused. All these ideas could not be combined into one all-embracing theory until the arrival of James Maxwell.

James Clerk Maxwell was a Scottish mathematician and physicist. In the 1860s, Maxwell was appointed the first professor of experimental physics at the new Cavendish Laboratory at Cambridge University. In 1873, he presented his theories, in which he was able to show clearly the mathematical relationship between electricity and magnetism that Faraday had first demonstrated in his experiments. Maxwell also observed that in an electromagnetic field, the lines of force radiated out from the electric charge at the speed of light. This proved what Faraday had suspected—that light is also a type of electromagnetic radiation. Maxwell also laid the foundations for radio and television by predicting that electrical signals could move in the air with a wavelike motion, just like ripples on the surface of a pond.

BACKGROUND TO MAXWELL'S WORK

In 1843, the British physicist James Joule had shown that electrical **energy** was changed into heat when a current passed through an electrical conductor. This resulted from the resistance of the conductor. One amp of current passing through one ohm of resistance made one **watt** of power. A few years later, in 1855, Wilhelm Weber, the professor of physics at Göttingen University in Germany, had shown that a particular relationship, or **ratio**, between electromagnet and electrostatic units was always a constant value (the same as the speed of light!). At Heidelberg University, Gustav Kirchhoff came up with some experimental results that showed that the speed of a signal along a telegraph wire was the same as the ratio of the electric charges worked out by Weber.

The Uses of Electricity

The value of electricity was quickly realized. Engineers and scientists developed many machines and devices that, since the mid-1800s, have changed peoples' lives drastically.

The "electro-magnetic telegraph" in Slough, England, on the Great Western Railway in August 1844 enabled important messages to be conveyed from Queen Victoria at Windsor Castle to her ministers in Westminster within 11 minutes! This caused great excitement at the time. The telegraph could be used by the public and inspected by them for a fee of one shilling, more than the average person could afford. The world's first paid telegrams were sent from here on May 16, 1843.

THE ELECTRIC TELEGRAPH

Telegraphy, or the transmission of messages along a conducting wire by pulses of electricity, had been a practical possibility since 1816. It was then that Sir Francis Ronalds first buried an insulated wire and sent telegraph messages over 325 feet (100 m). Ronalds showed his invention to the lords of the admiralty in London, but they were not interested.

The honor of being seen as the inventor of the electromagnetic telegraph finally went to Baron Schilling in Germany in 1832. However, the first commercial electric telegraph line was installed in London, England, in 1839. It ran between Paddington and West Drayton, a distance of 14 miles (22 km). By 1868, the telegraph system was in full commercial use in the United States and Europe.

MORSE CODE

The early telegraphs relied on a rotating needle at both the sending and receiving ends of the wire. The needle pivoted over a series of letters. When the needle at the sending end was pointed at a letter, the other end received a series of electrical pulses along the wire that made the needle at the receiving end move to the same position.

The early telegraphs were always breaking down, and a simpler method of sending messages was needed. The answer was given by Samuel Morse, who was a well-known artist and sculptor.

While traveling on a boat to Europe in 1829, Samuel Morse thought of a simple electrical **relay** that would attract and move a piece of iron in response to electric pulses sent along the telegraph wire. A pencil attached to the iron would put marks on some moving paper, and the marks could be translated later. It took Morse and his assistant, Alfred Vail, until 1836 to finish and **patent** his relay, or recorder. The recorder used a code of dots and dashes Morse and Vail invented to represent the alphabet. This was called the **Morse code**.

Samuel F. B. Morse with his electric relay and the marked, moving paper strip.

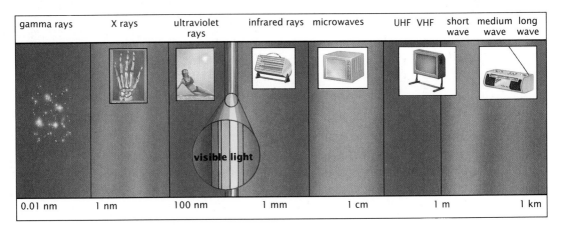

The electromagnetic spectrum

| gamma rays | X rays | ultraviolet rays | infrared rays | microwaves | UHF VHF | short wave | medium wave | long wave |

visible light

| 0.01 nm | 1 nm | 100 nm | 1 mm | 1 cm | 1 m | 1 km |

SENDING SIGNALS WITHOUT WIRES

In 1886, Heinrich Hertz, a German scientist, invented a machine to study the wavelike movement of electrical signals through the air. Maxwell's theory was confirmed by Hertz in 1887. Hertz's machine made a signal that constantly rose and fell, or **oscillated**. The signal's oscillations could be picked up, or detected, by a second circuit up to 60 feet (20 m) away, which was not connected to the oscillator!

Different types of radiation are detected by different means, but they are all electromagnetic waves and differ from each other only in their wavelength and **frequency**. We can only see a tiny part of the range, the visible spectrum.

THE WIRELESS TELEGRAPH

In 1893, Sir Oliver Lodge produced an improved receiver. He called his device a **coherer**, from "coherence," which means "to make sense." He also put it in a circuit with a recorder. The coded signals were detectable over a range of 810 feet (210 m) and the new "wireless"

system started to replace the electric telegraph in 1894.

By 1896, the range of the telegraph had been further improved to 3 miles (5 km) by Aleksandr Popov, a Russian scientist. Popov increased the ability of the coherer to pick up signals by fixing a metal rod, or antenna, to it.

Guglielmo Marconi

A young Italian named Guglielmo Marconi saw a newspaper report of Heinrich Hertz's discovery of wireless electric waves. He became very excited and decided to investigate further. He managed to build a **transmitter** to send Morse code signals and a **receiver** with an antenna that could receive these signals over long distances.

SIGNALS OVER WATER

In 1895, Guglielmo Marconi's invention was turned down by the Italian government, so he decided to approach the British government. He successfully demonstrated his radio telephony equipment to officers of the Royal Navy. They wanted to know if the invention worked over water, as they thought radio telephony would be a better way for ships to communicate with each other rather than the signal lamps and flags of that time. Marconi then successfully sent signals across the English Channel from England to France. In 1901, with the help of a huge antenna held in the sky by a kite, Marconi managed to send the first wireless signal across the Atlantic Ocean, from Cornwall in England to St. John's in Canada.

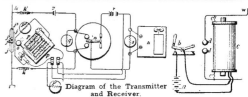

Diagram of the Transmitter and Receiver.

Here is an early photograph of Marconi and his radio transmitter. Every time the key was closed an extremely high voltage spark was made, and the energy was carried by a wire to an enormous antenna that transmitted the radio signal.

THE WIRELESS RADIO

The signals sent by Marconi's early equipment were limited to the high-speed dots and dashes of Morse code, which could only be understood by trained people. Marconi set up a company to develop his invention and broadcast human speech over the "wireless," later to be more popularly known as radio. The company's first public radio broadcast was in February 1920.

People were very interested in this new invention. Many bought a wireless receiver set made by Marconi's company. These sets had to be listened to through headphones. The wireless sets were powered by batteries that had to be charged once a week at the local shop!

Many people built their own simple receivers. These were called "crystal sets" because a crystal of the mineral galena was used in its circuit.

In 1920, KDKA in Pittsburgh, Pennsylvania, went on the air as the first commercial radio broadcast station in the United States. Within a few years, radio was established in many countries.

Glowing Gases

As early as 1838, Michael Faraday had noticed, during an experiment using a vacuum tube through which he put an electric current, that there was a glow covering the negative pole (or cathode) and a dark space separating the glow from the positive pole (or anode). It was difficult to make a good vacuum in Faraday's time, so nothing further was done to investigate this effect. In 1858, a German scientist named Julius Plücker, using improved vacuum tubes, described a "beautiful and mysterious green glow" on the cathode. These **cathode rays** could be deflected by nearby magnets.

Much has been learned about atoms since Von Helmholtz's time. We now know that an atom has a complicated structure made up of many small (subatomic) particles.

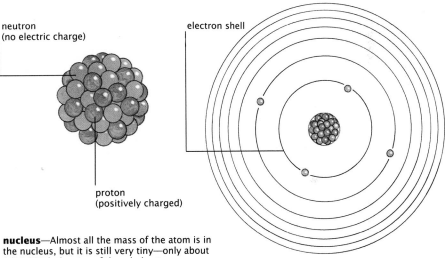

The structure of an atom

neutron (no electric charge)

electron shell

proton (positively charged)

nucleus—Almost all the mass of the atom is in the nucleus, but it is still very tiny—only about 1/10,000th the size of the whole atom.

Electrons (negatively charged) move around the nucleus in "shells" or layers. The number of shells and the number of electrons vary with each type of atom.

ELECTRICITY AND ATOMS

Hittorf's idea was taken further by the German physicist Hermann von Helmholtz, in 1881, when he said that electricity was like matter and that they both had an atomic structure. He believed that this theory was supported by the work of Michael Faraday and James Maxwell.

Meanwhile, Sir Joseph John Thomson had been carrying out work that enabled negative ions to be studied. In 1889, he discovered that these particles were 2,000 times lighter than atoms of hydrogen gas and succeeded in measuring the charge-to-mass ratio of the electron. J.J. Thomson's landmark experiment identified the electron as the first-known subatomic particle. He received the Nobel Prize for his discovery.

The Cathode-Ray Tube

In 1897, an Austrian physicist named Karl Braun made a vacuum tube that was flattened at one end. He coated the inside of the tube with a **fluorescent** substance that glowed when it was hit by a stream of electrons from a cathode. Braun found that the path of the electron stream could be altered by magnetic coils.

JOHN LOGIE BAIRD

John Logie Baird was an inventor who studied to be an engineer. He tried to make his fortune from a series of bizarre inventions, such as thermostatic socks that would keep your feet warm in winter and cool in summer, but none of these inventions became successful.

In 1923, Baird's thoughts turned to the new Marconi wireless and the broadcasts by the British Broadcasting Corporation. He wondered if it would be possible to send pictures using radio waves.

Baird had no money or backing and had to make his equipment from secondhand bits and pieces. He built a radio transmitter and receiver and, no doubt inspired by the "moving pictures," or movies, of the time, used a rotating mechanical scanner which had been invented by Paul Nipkow in 1884. As the scanner revolved, it divided the scene into a series of pictures, or frames. Baird's machine then transmitted the frames one-by-one by radio signals. Another scanner at the receiving end picked up the frames from the transmitting scanner.

By 1928, Baird had developed a primitive, mechanical color television. In 1930 he set up an experimental television network with the British Broadcasting Corporation.

BETTER TELEVISIONS

Baird's mechanical television was doomed to failure. By 1937, using the cathode-ray tube, Vladimir Zworykin in the U.S., Marconi's company with EMI in Great Britain, and Kenjiro Takayanagi in Japan, had produced electronic television systems. These televisions were far better than Baird's. Today, it is difficult to image life without the cathode-ray tube, which is used in televisions, computer monitors, electronic equipment like oscilloscopes, and radar and sonar equipment.

In the typical experimental cathode-ray tube shown here, the stream of electrons is produced by a heated coil. The electrons are directed and speeded up by the anode, which is at a high voltage, and travel to make the fluorescent material on the inside of the tube glow.

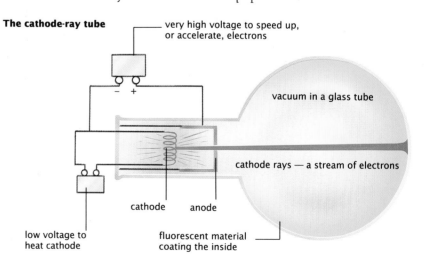

The cathode-ray tube

very high voltage to speed up, or accelerate, electrons

– +

vacuum in a glass tube

cathode rays — a stream of electrons

low voltage to heat cathode

cathode   anode

fluorescent material coating the inside

Electric Lighting

As far back as 1802, Humphry Davy had shown that strips of metal glowed brightly when a current was passed through them. Unfortunately, the metal also burned away and was useless as a light source. Later, in 1808, the carbon arc lamp was invented. The carbon also burned away in the air, but the light lasted longer and was very powerful. It was too bright to use in people's homes.

No progress was made with reliable electric lighting until 1838, when a thin rod of heated carbon was used in a vacuum for the first time. Many other people tried experimenting with this sort of arrangement, and many improvements were made to the carbon arc system, but it was finally put aside in favor of the **incandescent** lamp.

Here are four of Edison's early, experimental incandescent lamps. They all used various forms of carbon thread filaments in an evacuated glass tube.

INCANDESCENT LAMPS

The first incandescent lamps used a fine thread, or filament, of carbon in a vacuum. The invention is jointly credited to Thomas Edison, who worked independently in the U.S., and Sir Joseph Swan, who was working in Great Britain. Swan demonstrated his incandescent lamp in December 1878, and by October 1879, Edison had been able to run a light continuously for 45 hours.

In 1881, the two inventors formed the Edison and Swan United Electric Light Company. Their lamps made electric lighting very popular, and by the end of the century, the life of a light bulb had risen to 500 hours.

Improving the Light Bulb

The Siemens Company in Germany made the next advance in the efficiency of a light bulb when its scientists used the rare metal tantalum as a filament. In 1908, in the United States, tantalum was replaced by tungsten. This was because most metals become very soft when they are heated, but tungsten does not soften or break even at very high temperatures. At high temperatures, tungsten glows with a very bright light.

However, despite improved vacuums, the filaments still evaporated inside the bulbs. So experimenters tried putting various nonactive, or **inert**, gases inside the bulbs, instead of the vacuum. Argon proved to be the most suitable, as it stopped the filament from burning away and kept the bulb cooler than other gases.

STREET LIGHTING

A variety of gaseous-discharge lamps is widely used for street lights. The two gases that are used most often in street lighting are sodium vapor, which gives a yellow light, and mercury vapor, which gives a bluish-green light.

Here the street lighting is enhanced by a bewildering variety of advertising displays made from neon tubes. Other gases are mixed with the neon to give different colors.

GASEOUS-DISCHARGE LAMPS

Incandescent lamps are still the most common type of lighting in the home. However, they turn a lot of electric energy into heat instead of light. A more efficient lamp resulted from studying the glow, first seen by Michael Faraday, that is produced when an electric current discharges through a gas. Many different gases were tried in gaseous-discharge lamps. The first light of this kind was made in France in 1909 by Georges Claude, a French chemist and physicist, using neon gas. He used tubes to hold the gas, and this type of tube is in common use today. A neon tube gives a bright, orange-red light for a small current, with little wasted energy in the form of heat. Neon tubes were first used to make advertising displays in 1912.

ENERGY SAVING LAMPS

There is yet another type of lamp that works in the same way as gaseous-discharge lamps, but the inside of the tube or bulb is coated with a fluorescent material that glows. Although fluorescent lights were first invented before 1936, they were only developed as domestic lighting in the late 1940s. They are more expensive than incandescent bulbs but last about five years and only use one-eighth of the electricity for the same light output. A version developed in 1991 has no filament and promises to be an extremely efficient light bulb that will last indefinitely.

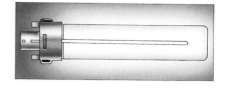

Fluorescent lamps like this are becoming common in the home.

Generating Electricity

In order to provide electricity for the many inventions that had been triggered by Michael Faraday's discoveries, machines needed to be invented to generate a steady supply. One of the earliest generators was invented by Hippolyte Pixii in Paris, France, in 1831. His machine, the first rotating electromagnetic generator, was turned by hand and produced an alternating current and very large electric shocks!

The designers of these early electrical machines seemed to think that the bigger the shock, the better the machine! The Great Exhibition of 1852 in London, England, awarded prizes for things like the strongest electromagnet or the best generator. Particular interest was shown in generating electricity to power arc lamps in lighthouses, and this led to the development of steam-driven generators.

STEAM-DRIVEN GENERATORS

In 1857, Frederick Holmes, with the advice of Michael Faraday, built a steam-driven generator weighing 2.2 tons. An improved version was used in the South Foreland lighthouse in England and was switched on in 1858. Holmes's design was further improved by 1867, and machines were installed in two other lighthouses. These remained in service for the next 33 years.

This early engraving shows Zénobe Gramme in his workshop putting the finishing touches to his dynamo.

THE DYNAMO-ELECTRIC GENERATOR

The electric current delivered by all the early generators was liable to vary in strength. The first machine to deliver a steady, continuous, and reversible current, was invented in France by Zénobe Gramme in 1871. It was called the **dynamo**.

The dynamo was remarkable because, unlike all generators up to then, it had no actual magnets in its design. Instead of magnets, part of the dynamo's output current was fed through large **field coils** to make the required magnetic field.

Gramme was also responsible for making the first alternators, which were introduced in 1878. The alternator turns energy from its rotation into electrical energy with an alternating current.

Public Power Generation

After the successes of the lighthouse generators, other arc lighting systems were installed in railroad yards, streets, and factories in the United States, France, and Great Britain. The demand for electric generating machinery started to grow, but as soon as the incandescent lamp was finally introduced, there was an explosion in demand.

THE SIEMENS BROTHERS

The Siemens family was very influential in the expansion of the electrical industry. There were four brothers born in Germany between 1816 and 1826. The eldest, Ernst, set up a telegraph factory in 1847, followed by factories in a number of European cities set up with his brother Karl. Wilhelm Siemens went to England in 1844. His early interest lay in electric telegraph cables laid under the sea. However, in 1877, he set up another factory to manufacture the recently invented dynamos. As an important industrialist, he was knighted and became Sir William Siemens.

The dynamo (or generator) changes mechanical, rotating energy into electrical energy. Some generators make alternating current, which flows rapidly first one way and then the other in a circuit. Other versions can make direct current, which flows in only one direction, just like a battery.

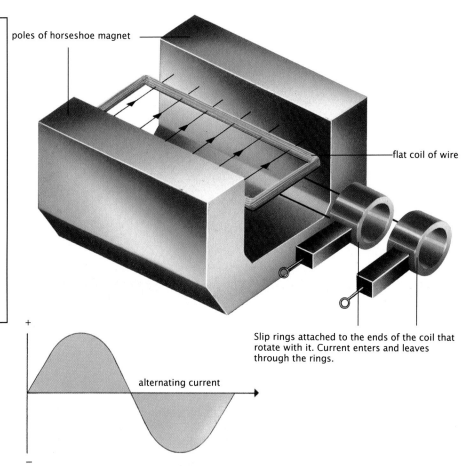

A generator

poles of horseshoe magnet

flat coil of wire

Slip rings attached to the ends of the coil that rotate with it. Current enters and leaves through the rings.

alternating current

A PUBLIC ELECTRICITY NETWORK

Thomas Edison was in the forefront of developing a public electricity network, and by the end of 1882, on New York's Pearl Street, 193 buildings with 4,000 lamps had been connected to Edison's "Jumbo" dynamos. At the same time, Edison also set up another network in England. This was in Holborn Viaduct, London. Many other companies were set up to sell electricity and, by the end of the 19th century, electricity was becoming commonplace.

SAVING POWER

Efficient generators were quickly developed. However, the system of wires used to carry the electricity from the generators to homes and factories wasted a lot of energy in the form of heat.

This problem was solved by the introduction of the modern transformer, which was invented between 1882 and 1885. This transformer was based, like so many electrical things, on Michael Faraday's discoveries about induction and relied on the alternator and alternating current. The transformer was used to increase the voltage to the wires. This meant that the same power could be transmitted with a lower current and much less heat loss.

A CONFUSION OF NETWORKS

Many different companies were involved in the new electrical distribution systems, so different machines were working to different standards. Alternating-current systems gradually took over, as there was less power loss during transmission than there was with the older, direct-current systems, which had used batteries. In the United States, the supply of electricity was in the hands of private companies, all operating with the same standards. In Great Britain, in 1925, all the supply companies were combined into the Central Electricity Generating Board with over 80 separate generating companies using 17 different frequencies of alternating current!

Transformers like this alter the voltages of the grid system from 400,000 volts to 275,000 volts.

GENERATING STATIONS

By 1960, the early, small steam-driven generators had been replaced by large machines that could produce huge amounts of energy. The steam was made in boilers fired by coal, oil, or natural gas. When these natural fossil fuels were burned, the energy released was converted to electricity. A **national power grid**, or framework of interlinking cables, was put up to deliver electric power all over the country and to share electricity made in different places.

Electricity has to be switched to where it is needed, and these huge circuit breakers are used to route electricity from the hydroelectric generating plant in Bonneville, Idaho, to the national grid system.

Alternative Energy Sources

For some time, people have worried about burning fossil fuels like coal, oil, and gas to make electricity. Fossil fuels were deposited millions of years ago, and they are in limited supply. The power stations are not very efficient, as they only get about 40 percent of the possible energy from fossil fuels. The rest is wasted. Recently, people have realized that when we burn fossil fuels, we put large amounts of carbon dioxide and poisonous gases into the air. This is having a damaging effect on the plant and animal life on Earth and on the air we breathe. Scientists are now working to find better sources of electricity.

WIND AND SUN

Energy from wind power is also being researched, and there are now a few "wind farms" where huge propellers are driven around by the wind to generate energy. A very efficient source of electrical energy is the sun. Sunlight can be directly converted into electrical energy. This is proving successful in countries where there is plenty of sunshine. The most powerful solar energy plant was built in 1982 in California.

This wind farm is in California. The stable, warm climate and the physical location of the farm ensures there is a steady wind for most of the year to turn the propellers to generate electricity.

HYDROELECTRIC POWER

An excellent source of energy for making electricity is running water. The first person to make hydro-electric power was Aristide Bergès in 1869 in the French Alps. Since then, hydroelectric plants have been built all over the world and have often depended on building a suitable dam to store the needed water, such as the Hoover Dam located on the Colorado River.

The movement of the sea is also being used in tidal-power plants, which use the ebb and flow of the tides. Wave-power generators use the energy associated with the motion of waves.

Nuclear Power

Another alternative power source is nuclear power. Enormous amounts of energy are released when the central core, or nucleus, of a uranium atom is split. The first **atomic pile** was made in Chicago, Illinois, by Enrico Fermi and other scientists in 1942. This pile enabled uranium nuclei to be split, a process known as **fission** in a controlled way. The first nuclear power station was built in the U.S. in 1951. Expensive programs were started to produce similar power stations all over the world, particularly in Great Britain, France, and the former Soviet Union.

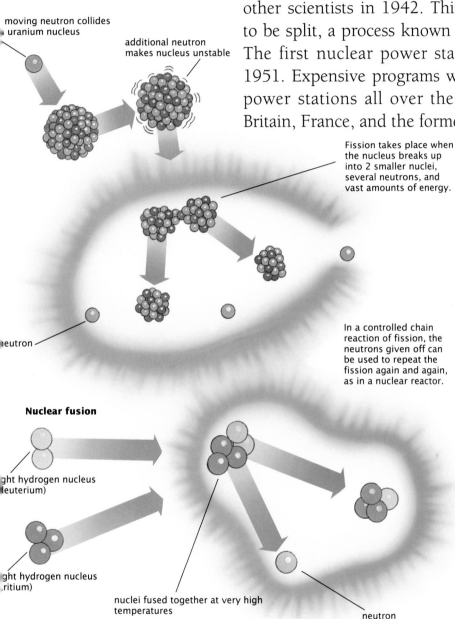

Nuclear fission using uranium

moving neutron collides uranium nucleus

additional neutron makes nucleus unstable

Fission takes place when the nucleus breaks up into 2 smaller nuclei, several neutrons, and vast amounts of energy.

neutron

In a controlled chain reaction of fission, the neutrons given off can be used to repeat the fission again and again, as in a nuclear reactor.

Nuclear fusion

ght hydrogen nucleus (deuterium)

ght hydrogen nucleus (ritium)

nuclei fused together at very high temperatures

neutron

Fusion produces a helium nucleus, a single neutron, and vast amounts of energy, but no dangerous radioactive products.

PROBLEMS WITH NUCLEAR POWER

Nuclear power is proving to be less and less popular as time goes on. It produces a lot of dangerous, **radioactive** waste products that are difficult to dispose of safely. The waste has to be stored for many thousands of years, until it is no longer radioactive. If anything goes wrong, the lives of millions of people can be threatened by radioactive **fallout**, as happened when the Chernobyl plant in the Ukraine caught fire in 1986. However, the economies of many countries still depend on nuclear power for energy.

NUCLEAR FUSION

Today, nuclear power comes from nuclear fission, but scientists are working on nuclear fusion, or the forcing of hydrogen atoms together. Fusion is what powers the sun and, while fusion also frees large amounts of energy, it does so without creating any harmful radioactive wastes. The fusion process can only be done at temperatures of millions of degrees Celsius. The difficulty is in making these high temperatures and containing them. In 1957, the physicist John Lawson produced the theory for a controlled fusion process. Scientists are still working on this process.

The Electronic Revolution

In 1904 Sir John Fleming invented the vacuum tube rectifier or **diode**. Consisting of a filament and a plate (cathode and anode), this two-element vacuum tube could convert alternating current into direct current. It could also serve as a "detector" in simple radio sets.

The diode was developed further in the United States in 1907 by Lee De Forest, who put in a third electrode. This triode (which means three electrodes), called a grid, was able to increase, or **amplify**, signal levels. So, with the help of a loudspeaker, the sounds produced by a radio could be heard by anyone within the room, rather than only on a pair of headphones.

The ENIAC computer was one of the largest of the early computers. It occupied a room 30 feet by 50 feet (10 m by 16 m) and took four people to operate. Today's desktop personal computers are more sophisticated and faster.

GIANT COMPUTERS

Today, electricity and electronics are everywhere in our society. The diode and the amplifier are the foundation on which today's massive electronics industry is still based. The first electron tubes were bulky and fragile and gave off a lot of heat. The first commercial computers, although less powerful than todays PCs, used thousands of tubes and took up the volume of an average-sized house.

SEMICONDUCTORS

Today's electronic devices no longer depend on vacuum tube technology. Electronic devices are much smaller due to the discovery of a new class of materials. Michael Faraday noticed, back in 1839, that some substances conducted electricity better in one direction than the other. In 1929, these materials were called **semiconductors** by the American physicist Felix Bloch because they sometimes behaved like conductors and sometimes like insulators. This depends on a variety of factors, such as their temperature or how much light fell on them.

One of the most important semiconductors is silicon which, in the compound sand, is one of the most common substances on Earth. In 1948, three scientists in the U.S. made a breakthrough. They were John Bardeen, Walter Brattain, and William Shockley. They learned how to blend, or **dope**, semiconductors with minute amounts of other substances to form crystals with new electronic properties. These crystals could be made into **transistors**, which were tiny versions of vacuum tube diodes and triodes.

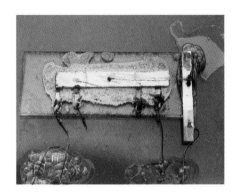

The first integrated circuit (originally known as a single-crystal circuit) was invented by Jack Kilby of Texas Instruments in 1958.

This device packs the entire central processing unit of a computer onto one tiny silicon chip. The square pads on the outside are used to connect the device to power supplies and to other circuits.

SILICON CHIPS

Since 1958, scientists have learned to etch semiconductors with acid to make very tiny electronic devices. Millions of transistor switches, diodes, or amplifiers can be made on one chip of silicon and then connected together to make an integrated, or all-in-one, circuit. The integrated circuit brought about a modern technological explosion to rival the first industrial revolution. Every year, the devices are made smaller, more powerful, and faster.

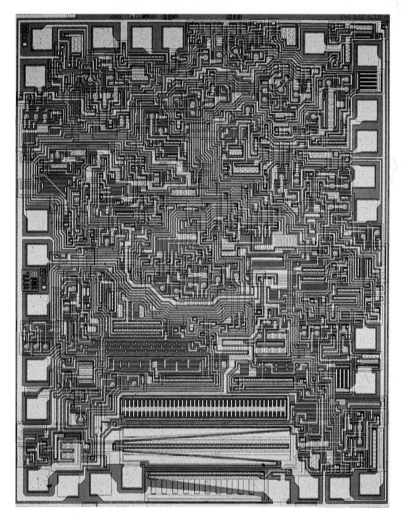

Electricity in the Future

In 1954, a solar-powered battery was developed using the **photovoltaic cell** discovered by Antoine Becquerel in 1839. The photovoltaic cell changes the energy of light to a low voltage electric current. The first cells were very inefficient, but since 1987, new techniques have increased their efficiency. Solar batteries now provide extra power in sunny parts of the world, as well as powering watches, calculators, and scientific instruments in space.

FUSION POWER STATIONS

Since John Lawson produced a good theoretical base for creating nuclear power through controlled nuclear fusion in 1957, some successful research has been achieved. Very high temperatures have been reached at the European Center for Nuclear Research (CERN) and, in 1983, at the Massachusetts Institute of Technology (MIT). Temperatures around 100 million K need to be maintained over long periods of time if the controlled fusion process is to succeed.

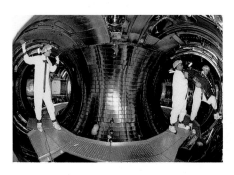

Scientists are checking the inside of the Tokomak Fusion Test Reactor. Fusion occurs at temperatures like those found in the sun, and strong magnetic fields are used to contain the hot gases to keep the heat away from the walls of the reactor.

SUPERCONDUCTORS

These enormous temperatures cannot be contained by just any material. They have to be contained within strong magnetic fields which are created by passing very high currents through coils of wire. Because these currents need to be so high, scientists had to develop **superconductors**.

Superconductivity was discovered in 1911 by the Dutch physicist Heike Kamerlingh Onnes. He found that metals that were immersed in liquid helium, which is as cold as -454°F (-269°C), lost most of their resistance to electric current. So, a thin wire could carry an enormous current as long as it remained at that low temperature.

SUPERCONDUCTIVE CERAMICS

Using superconductive material in other ways would be useful and save wasted power. However, the very low temperatures create difficulties. In 1986, Alex Müller and J. George Bednorz in Zurich, Switzerland, discovered superconductivity in some ceramic materials at -373°F (-238°C). In 1987, scientists in both

The *Skylab* space station had four solar battery arrays at the top for the Apollo Telescope Mount. It should have two further arrays at the bottom, but one is missing.

the United States and China found superconductivity at only -292°F (180°C), which is a much more practical temperature.

Scientists are now hoping to find materials that will become superconductive near 32°F (0°C). If this breakthrough occurs, the whole technology of electricity will, once again, be turned on its head.

Important Dates

1300 B.C. Magnetic stones are discovered in Asia Minor.

c 600 B.C. Thales comments on the attractive power of amber.

c A.D. 1100 Compasses made with magnetic lodestones are widely used.

1269 Petrus Peregrinus writes *De Magnete*, a study of magnetism.

1500s Sailors observe that magnetic north and true north vary.

1600s William Gilbert writes a study on magnets, and invents an electroscope and the terms *electricity* and *magnetic rays*.

c 1650 Otto von Guericke invents the first electrical machine.

1660 Robert Boyle discovers magnetism does not need air to work.

1729 Stephen Gray discovers conductivity and induction.

1733 Charles Du Fay discovers some materials act as insulators.

1746 Pieter van Musschenbroek invents the Leyden jar to store electricity.

c 1750 William Watson discovers the effect of completing an electrical circuit.

1752 Benjamin Franklin relates lightning to electricity and invents the lightning rod. He suggests the idea of positive and negative electricity.

1767 Joseph Priestly discovers conductivity.

1770s Henry Cavendish discovers resistance and potential, and studies the capacitor for storing a charge.

1780s Charles Coulomb invents the torsion balance to measure the force between charged particles.

1780 Luigi Galvani discovers electricity in living things.

1792 Giovanni Fabbroni discovers the oxidizing effect of electricity.

1800 Alessandro Volta builds a voltaic pile—the first battery.

1802 Coulomb publishes his laws of attraction and repulsion of positive and negative charges.

c 1810 Humphry Davy invents the carbon arc lamp.

1816 Sir Francis Ronalds sends the first telegraphic message.

1819 Hans Christian Ørsted discovers the connection between electricity and magnetism.

1820 André Ampère devises distinctions between electrostatics and electric currents, and current and voltage. He invents the galvanometer to demonstrate them.

1821 Michael Faraday invents the first electric motor.

1825 Georg Ohm shows the exact relationship between voltage, current, and resistance.

1831 Faraday generates direct current and alternating current, and invents the alternator and the transformer.

1832 Faraday proves that all forms of electricity are the same. He devises new terms—*electrolysis, cathode, anode,* and *ion.* His work leads to a massive expansion in electrical machinery.

1837 Samuel Morse patents his telegraphic relay and Morse code.

1839 Antoine Becquerel invents the photovoltaic cell.

1857 Frederick Holmes builds the first large steam generator.

1858 Julius Plücker discovers cathode rays and the fact that they can be deflected by magnets.

1869 Aristide Bergès sets up the first hydroelectric plant.

1871 Zénobe Gramme invents the dynamo electric generator.

1873 James Maxwell publishes mathematical equations to prove that light is a form of electro-magnetic radiation.

1876 Alexander Graham Bell sends the first telephone message.

1877 Thomas Edison invents the phonograph.

1878–1879 Joseph Swan and Thomas Edison independently invent the light bulb.

1881 Hermann von Helmholtz suggests that electricity has an atomic structure.

1886–1887 Heinrich Hertz makes an oscillator to confirm his findings on light and discovers radio waves.

1895 Guglielmo Marconi invents a wireless transmitter and receiver that can send Morse code messages by radio waves.

1897 J.J. Thomson discovers the electron and determines its charge-to-mass ratio.

1901 Marconi sends a wireless signal from Great Britain to the United States.

1904 John Fleming constructs the first diode vacuum tube.

1906 Lee De Forest builds a triode, which amplifies signals.

1909 Georges Claude invents the neon light.

1911 Superconductivity is discovered by Heike Kamerlingh Onnes.

1920 The first public radio broadcast of speech is made.

1928 John Logie Baird invents a mechanical television.

1929 Felix Bloch names a class of materials *semiconductors*. Silicon is an example of a semiconductor.

1937 Electronic televisions based on the cathode-ray tube are produced in the United States, Great Britain, and Japan.

1942 Enrico Fermi builds the first nuclear pile in Chicago.

1948 John Bardeen, Walter Brattain, and William Shockley learn how to dope semiconductors to produce transistors.

1954 The first large-scale nuclear power station is built in Obninsk, Russia.

1954 The solar powered battery is developed.

1957 John Lawson produces a workable theory for controlled nuclear fusion.

1960s Giant generators were introduced for electricity generation.

1983 Very high temperatures for nuclear fusion are achieved at the Massachusetts Institute of Technology.

1986 Alex Müller and J. George Bednorz discover superconductivity in ceramic materials.

Glossary

alternating current (AC): current that regularly changes direction in a circuit

alternator: a machine that generates alternating current by rotating a coil between poles of a magnet

ampere/amp: the SI (International System) unit of electric current. One amp is equal to the current flowing when one watt is being produced at one volt.

amplify: to boost or increase a signal or sound

anode: a positive electrode that attracts electrons. Electrons enter a battery through the anode.

atom: the smallest particle of an element that still has the properties of that element. Atoms are made up of negatively charged electrons and a nucleus of neutrons and positively charged protons.

atomic pile: a device containing uranium and used to control a fission reaction. The nuclear pile forms the core of a nuclear reactor.

attract: to pull toward itself

carbon arc: a flash of bright light that arches, or arcs, between two pieces of carbon to complete a circuit when a current is switched on

cathode: a negative electrode that repels electrons. Electrons leave a battery through the cathode.

cathode ray: a stream of electrons given off by a cathode in a vacuum when connected to an electric current. If a cathode ray is focused on a fluorescent screen, the screen will glow.

cell: a device for producing electricity by a chemical reaction, such as a battery

charged: having an imbalance of electrical charges

circuit: a complete circular route or pathway. An electric circuit makes a path through which electricity can flow.

coherer: a device that converted radio waves into usable current by passing them through conducting granules

compass: an instrument that shows direction by always pointing north

conduct: to allow electricity to pass through

conductivity: the ability of a material to allow electricity to pass through

conductors: materials that allow electricity to pass easily through them

contacts: points where wires connect to a circuit

cross section: the exposed surface of something that has been cut straight through, such as the end of a wire

deflect: to turn or push aside

diode: a glass vacuum with a heater and two (*di-* means two) electrodes. Current can flow only one way through a tube.

direct current (DC): current flowing continuously in one direction only

discharge: to give off or receive electrons, creating an electric output

dope: to introduce a small amount of impurity (such as another chemical) into a semiconductor

dynamo: any rotating machine in which mechanical energy is converted into electrical energy

electrodes: the plates in batteries or capacitors through which current enters or leaves

electrodynamic: describing movement that results from electric currents or magnets

electrolysis: separating a liquid into its chemical parts by using a current of electricity

electrolytic effect: any effect resulting from electrolysis. Metals (such as copper) can be coated with a thin layer of another metal (such as silver) by electrolysis.

electromagnet: a magnet created when an electric current is passed through a coil of wire wound around an iron or steel bar

electromotive force: the potential difference produced by a battery or generator that makes current flow

electron: one of the subatomic particles. Electrons carry a negative electrical charge.

electronic: anything relating to the controlled use of electrons

electroscope: a device for detecting electricity and determining whether the charge is positive or negative

element: a substance that cannot be divided into simpler parts by a chemical reaction

energy: the ability to do work. Energy takes many different forms and can change from one form to another. Energy cannot be created or destroyed—only changed or exchanged.

evaporate: to disappear, usually referring to a liquid becoming a gas or a vapor. The heat of the sun makes water in a puddle evaporate.

experiment: a controlled test of an idea or a theory

extract: to take something out of something else

fallout: clouds of radioactive dust resulting from a nuclear explosion

field coil: coiled wire used to produce a magnetic field in a dynamo

fission: the process by which the heavy nucleus of an atom is split into two or more lighter nuclei. This process releases huge amounts of energy.

fluorescent: glowing with light when bombarded by electrons

frequency: the number of times a movement, or cycle, repeats itself in one second. The unit in which frequency is measured is the hertz.

friction: the force that acts to resist motion, as when two surfaces slide over each other. Friction often creates a release of energy, such as heat or static electricity.

fusion: the process by which two atomic nuclei collide and combine together to form a heavier nucleus. This process releases vast amounts of energy and occurs naturally in the sun and other stars.

generate: to bring into existence or to cause something to happen

gravity: gravitational force or the force of attraction between two objects. Unless the objects are very large (such as planets), the force is very small.

incandescent: glowing without burning. The filament in an incandescent lamp glows when a current passes through it.

induce: to produce an effect or cause a reaction

inert: nonreactive; describes a substance that does not react with any other substance

insight: a sudden understanding or idea

insulator: any material that does not allow electricity to pass through it. Materials such as plastic or rubber have a high resistance to electricity, so they are used to insulate electrical wires.

ion: an atom that has been charged positively (by removing an electron) or negatively (by adding an electron)

like poles: two magnetic poles that push apart or repel each other

magnet: a bar or horseshoe of metal that has the power to attract certain other metals

magnetic field: the area of magnetic force that radiates out from a magnet

magnetic north: the location on the Earth's surface at which the north pole of a compass points

magnetism: the ability of certain objects to attract or repel certain other objects

Morse code: a system used for signaling in which each letter of the alphabet is given an agreed pattern of dots and dashes. The code can be used as flashes of light or pulses of electricity.

national power grid: a network of interconnecting power cables allowing power to be distributed over a whole country

negative: describing the electric charge of electrons

nerve: a chain of small units, or neurons, that carry "messages" between the brain of an animal and the rest of the body. The "messages" are made up of electrical pulses.

ohm: the SI unit of resistance; one volt produces a current of one amp when the resistance is one ohm.

opposite poles: two magnetic poles that attract each other

oscillate: to swing from side to side or to-and-fro

oxidize: to combine with oxygen

parallel: extending in the same direction and always the same distance apart

patent: an official document that registers an invention and gives the owner sole right to develop and sell the invention

photovoltaic cell: a device that produces an electric current when exposed to light

pivot: to turn freely around another object

poles: the points on a magnet at which its magnetic force is strongest. Every magnet has two poles—those that seek magnetic north and those that seek magnetic south.

positive: describing the electric charge of protons

potential: referring to the energy difference between the negative and positive terminals of a battery or generator

radio telephony: a system of transmitting and receiving voice messages using radio waves

radio waves: invisible electromagnetic waves that travel freely in space and can be produced by a transmitter

radioactive: describing unstable atomic nuclei that break up into different nuclei and give off rays, known as radioactivity. The nuclei give off rays until they become stable, which can take anything from seconds to hundreds of years.

ratio: the number of times that something occurs in relation to something else

rays of magnetic force: lines that show the direction of a magnetic field around a magnet

reaction: a change resulting from the interaction of chemicals

receiver: a machine or device that receives and processes signals, such as radio waves

relay: a device used when a small current is required to switch a larger current on and off

repel: to drive away or push back

repulsion: the state of being driven away or pushed back

resin: sticky substances produced by some plants. Resins often become solid and stonelike.

self-induction: the creation of an electromotive force in a coil of current-carrying wire when the current changes

semiconductors: materials whose ability to resist electrical current is between that of conductors and insulators. Their resistance can be changed by altering their temperature or adding other chemicals.

static electricity: electricity made by rubbing or friction

superconductors: a class of material that has no electrical resistance at very low temperatures

theory: an explanation, supported by evidence, of a natural phenomenon

thermoelectric junctions: two dissimilar metals joined together

transformer: a device used to change the voltage of an alternating current

transistor: an electrical device that is able to control or amplify the flow of an electric current

transmitter: a machine used to process and send (transmit) signals, such as radio waves

uniform: completely even

vacuum pump: a pump used to evacuate, or extract, all the air from a container, thus creating a vacuum

voltage: potential difference. The unit by which potential difference is measured is the volt, named after Alessandro Volta.

watt: the SI unit of power that measures the rate of doing work or rate of change of energy

BIBLIOGRAPHY

Bailey, Mark W. *Electricity.* Raintree Steck-Vaughn, Austin, 1988

Cash, Terry. *Electricity and Magnets.* Watts, New York, 1989

Davis, Kay and Oldsfield, Wendy. *Electricity and Magnetism.* Raintree Steck-Vaughn, Austin, 1991

Gutnick, Martin J. *Electricity: From Faraday to Solar Generators.* Watts, New York, 1986

Johnston, Tom. *Electricity Turns the World On!* Gareth Stevens Inc., Milwaukee, 1987

Index